A Pictorial History
of Tucker County, West Virginia

Moving of courthouse records from St. George to Parsons.
Photo at Parsons, looking northeast on Second Street.

Contributor Chris Kidwell

McClain Printing Company
Parsons, WV
www.mcclainprinting.com
2011

International Standard Book Number 0-87012-773-X
Library of Congress Control Number 2011937126
Printed in the United States of America
Copyright © 2011 by McClain Printing Company
Parsons, West Virginia
All Rights Reserved
2011

Tucker County, West Virginia
Established March 7, 1856[1]

Tucker County, West Virginia, with its vast array of beautiful mountains and valleys, is a county rich in history and family tradition. Established over 150 years ago, the collection of business leaders, artisans, laborers, homemakers, educators and others who have either grown up in the hills of Tucker County or made their lives there enable one to have a montage of photographs detailing the people and the times. With Tucker County having three published county histories[2] each covering a different span of time, the need for another in the year 2011 seemed moot. However, a pictorial history displaying photographs from over a hundred years ago to today was something that McClain Printing Company was interested in from the day that Chris Kidwell came to MPC's offices with the idea. Along with Chris came hundreds of photos that he had in his personal collection or had purchased at auctions and websites. These along with other contributions make up this phenomenal collection of historic photos.

This county history is created by photographs and postcards depicting life featuring Parsons, St. George, Hambleton, Hendricks, Thomas, and Davis including Canaan Valley. There are additional photos of Auviltown, Jenningston, Laneville, William, etc. All of these towns have families, businesses, and areas that contributed to living in Tucker County. From the Parsons Tannery and Elmer Lipscomb's to the Buxton Landstreet Building and Blackwater Falls, the intent of this history is to document the life and times of Tucker County through photographs and to remind those who have a connection to this area of memorable people and places which make up who they are today.

Additional photos were submitted by various individuals who were generous enough to contribute them for this publication. All photos are captioned with the names of the contributor unless the contributor wished to remain anonymous. We apologize in advance for any misnamed persons or places. In most cases, we only had the written words on the back (or front) of photos to label each picture. Some photos had no description at all but are thought or known to be of the Tucker County area. In some instances, we received the same photo from different contributors. In that case, we used the one which was submitted first to MPC.

We hope you enjoy this trip down memory lane.
We did and we are delighted to share the journey with you.

---

[1] *History of Tucker County* by Homer Floyd Fansler, McClain Printing Company, 1962.
[2] *History of Tucker County* by Hu Maxwell, *History of Tucker County* by Homer Floyd Fansler, *History of Tucker County* by Cleta Long—all published by McClain Printing Company.

Additional contributors to *A Pictorial History of Tucker County* ~~

Ray and Lucille Adams
Ernest Arhar
Bruce Auvil
James and Robert Auvil
Jane H. Barb
Jeffrey and Anita Barb
Don Barr
Bill and Retha Bilby
Steve Bodkins
Jean H. Burns
Phyllis Carr
Evelyn Chaney
Anetta Shahan Creekmore
Madonna DiBacco
Bill and Linda Evick
Dixie Goff Gutmann
Flossie Hardy
Hinkle Funeral Home
Betty Knicely
McClain Printing Company
Susan Meyer
Elmer "Slim" Moreland
Delain Mullenax
Paul Nestor
Parsons Volunteer Fire Department
Jane Pifer
David and Rita Roberts
Faith Smith Robinson
Jim Root
Shaffer
Jeannette Shahan
Ed Simmons Family
Keith Simmons
Mariwyn McClain Smith
Annie Snyder
Chris Stadelman
Veronica Tekavec Staron
David and Wilda Strahin
Etta Sturms Family
Alice Tekavec
Frances Tekavec
Kim Michael Wilfong

Table of Contents

Acknowledgements

As a native Tucker Countian, I have always had a keen interest in the history of the county and have spent years collecting and purchasing photographs of the area. From Shaver's Mountain where my mother, Dessie C. Judy Kidwell, was raised, to Davis, where my father, John Wade Kidwell was born, to Parsons, where my siblings and I went to school, I have gathered as much information as possible on the people and places that made Tucker County home.

Some of my photo collection came from family archives; the rest I found through auctions, internet sites, postcard collectors, yard and estate sales and individuals I have known from my youth. My maternal grandparents, Isom and Gertie Judy, had a large postcard collection. I owe my love of history to them.

There are friends and individuals I would like to thank with my deepest gratitude and appreciation for their assistance throughout the time that I have been working on this project. I would first like to thank James Clark West of Morgantown, for hauling me around and finding me old photos in his travels. I would also like to extend my appreciation to Jane H. Barb, Bill and Retha Bilby, Don Barr, Flossie Hardy, Steve Bodkins, Jessie Sponaugle Bodkin, Dave and Wilda Strahin, Bill and Shirley Judy, Tom Bonner, Eldon Plaugher, Kim Michael Wilfong, Lisa Mauzy Wilfong, Bert and Ernie Price, Everette Price, Bessie Mae Kidwell Munson and especially my parents, Wade and Dess Kidwell, and my grandparents, Isom and Gertie Judy. Hopefully, I didn't forget anyone and I thank you all for your knowledge and help.

Most of all, a very special thanks to McClain Printing Company for making this pictorial history possible. Ken and Shelly, thank you very much for your patience and ability in making the book a reality.

To the readers, please forgive any mistakes or incorrect identifications. I tried to the best of my ability to make sure that descriptions of people, places and dates were correct. If you happen to know names of unidentified persons, please contact the publisher or myself so that corrections can be made when the book is, hopefully, reprinted some day. The addition of family photos helped to create a more diversifed book and I want to thank those families for their contributions. I hope that future generations will enjoy this book as we all have Maxwell's, Fansler's and Long's histories of Tucker County.

Chris Kidwell
September 16, 2011

Parsons, West Virginia

Established June 12, 1893 as an incorporated town
Established February 18, 1907 as an incorporated city[3]

View of Parsons from Quality Hill, 1912-1920, postcard.
Courtesy of Chris Kidwell.

Parsons postcard. Area is visible where St. John's United Methodist Church now stands. This part of Parsons was once called "Chaseboro" and had its own post office in the 1890s.
Courtesy of Chris Kidwell.

[3]*History of Tucker County* by Homer Floyd Fansler, McClain Printing Company, 1962.

View from Moose Hill,
First Street, Parsons.
Courtesy of Chris Kidwell.

Parsons, postcard.
Courtesy of Chris Kidwell.

Dirt Streets. Parting of the ways, Parsons, postcard. Chestnut Street, *left*; Main Street, *right*. Taken by Broadwater Art Studio.
Courtesy of Chris Kidwell.

View of Pulp Mill Bottom, Parsons, 1909. Photo by Broadwater Art Studio.
Courtesy of Chris Kidwell.

Parsons, W. Va.

Parsons was incorporated in 1893 and named for Ward Parsons, Sr., owner of most of the land on which the town now stands. It is 1,650 feet in altitude and its 1960 population is 1,773. The first settler in Parsons was John Crouch, Sr., (1720-1788) and he settled there in 1766, as the first settler in Tucker County as well as the first in Parsons. He moved to Huttonsville in 1772, and in 1788, while strolling around barefooted in his yard, one moonlit night, was bitten by a rattlesnake from which he died.

Parsons Marker, postcard.
Courtesy of Chris Kidwell.

"John Crouch, pioneer settler, established "tomahawk rights" here in 1766, but the town was not incorporated until 1893. Here Shaver's Fork and Blackwater unite to form the Cheat River. Hu Maxwell, the historian, lived near."

First Street in Parsons in 1910

Tucker County Fair Program -- 1960.
Courtesy of Chris Kidwell.

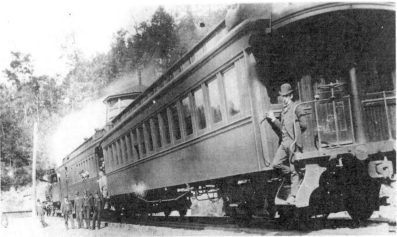

Watering tank between Hambleton and Parsons, Western Maryland Railroad, 1908, postcard.
Courtesy of Kim Michael Wilfong.

William Minear and friends, night of Sept. 10, 1906, hunting party, head of Haddox at Moore.
Courtesy of Chris Kidwell.

October 24, 1920, postcard.
Courtesy of Kim Michael Wilfong.

William "Billy" (1856-1933) and Elizabeth Canon (1872-1937) Knotts.
Courtesy of Delain Mullenax.

Unknown, Parsons.
Courtesy of Chris Kidwell.

View of Parsons from Quality Hill, postcard.
Courtesy of Chris Kidwell.

Ralph and Betty Stewart, July 18, 1949. He owned a furniture and appliance store in Parsons; she was a beautician.
Courtesy of Mariwyn McClain Smith.

View of Parsons looking westward--courthouse *on the left, bank in the middle (brick)*, opera house *far back (stone)*, postcard.
Courtesy of Chris Kidwell.

Judy Baer (Mullennex), Parsons High School, Class of 1953.
Courtesy of Mariwyn McClain Smith.

View of Parsons Shaver's Fork River in foreground, postcard.
Courtesy of Chris Kidwell.

Low water, Blackfork River, Parsons, 1908, postcard.
Courtesy of Chris Kidwell.

Photo of a "moonshine" whiskey still. Unknown if actually taken in Tucker County, but good example of what an actual working still looked like.
Courtesy of Chris Kidwell.

Lloyd Hansford Building -- (later Opera House), First Street, Parsons, razed in 2009.
Courtesy of Chris Kidwell.

Parsons, postcard.
Courtesy of Chris Kidwell.

Looking toward Parsons from Alum Hill, postcard.
Courtesy of Chris Kidwell.

Looking east, postcard, Parsons.
Courtesy of Chris Kidwell.

Unknown, photo from Etta Sturms family. Parsons World War I soldier from Holly Meadows.
Courtesy of Chris Kidwell.

Going toward St. George. View below Parsons, 1949, postcard. Holly Meadows and Moss Bridge.
Courtesy of Chris Kidwell.

Dogwood in bloom at Mandy Hollow Grade. U.S. Rt. 219 and Western Maryland Railroad grade above Moore, postcard.
Courtesy of Chris Kidwell.

Dale Crosten, former sheriff of Tucker County serving as parade marshall for Tucker County Fair. Parsons, photo.
Courtesy of Chris Kidwell.

1940s -- Looking at Bretz, at the base of Turkey Knob. Note road to Blackman Flats, postcard.
Courtesy of Chris Kidwell.

Parsons photo, going onto
Pennsylvania Avenue
toward Bretz.
Courtesy of Shaffer.

Front Street, Parsons. Tucker County Bank,
far right. Notice the street signs.
Courtesy of Chris Kidwell.

Intersection at Main and First streets, Ours Garage - Western Maryland Railroad Depot, photo.
Courtesy of Jane H. Barb.

Harness Judy,
1890-1909, killed
on Cheat Mountain
at a lumber camp.
Died in his brother,
Isom Judy's, arms.
Also a brother to
Glen Judy.
*Courtesy of
Chris Kidwell.*

Parsons 1950s, taken from First Street
and Main, Chrysler-Plymouth Ours-
Kee Garage *at the right*. Hinebaugh's
Restaurant was across from Ours-
Kee Garage, postcard.
Courtesy of Chris Kidwell.

Courthouse, corner of First and Walnut streets, Parsons.
Courtesy of Jane H. Barb.

Tucker County Courthouse showing new $5,000 clock. Postcard dated Sept. 18, 1928, Parsons.
Courtesy of Chris Kidwell.

Taken from the hill, Battle Street, before Parsons High School was built, postcard.
Courtesy of Chris Kidwell.

Main Street, Parsons. Hugh Harsh, Jessie S. Nestor, Willard Sturm, photo.
Courtesy of Chris Kidwell.

Mike and Hattie Vance Mauzy.
Courtesy of Chris Kidwell.

_____ and Hattie Vance Mauzy.
Courtesy of Chris Kidwell.

1913 -- R.W. Evans, Harness Shop, Parsons, photo.
Courtesy of Jane H. Barb.

Old Ford garage *on left* by the bridge on Railroad Street, Parsons in winter, photo.
Courtesy of Jane H. Barb.

Mary Wamsley Hansford and Linus standing at the entrance to the driveway. Old Moose Building *in background*, (Lloyd Hansford home) Parsons.
Courtesy of Chris Kidwell.

Moving courthouse records from St. George to Parsons
looking northeast on Second Street. *Photo courtesy of Chris Kidwell.*
"Parsons became the county seat of Tucker County, by law, August 7, 1893, although the records and other paraphernalia had been unlawfully removed from Saint George five days previous to that date." [4]

[4] *History of Tucker County* by Homer Floyd Fansler, McClain Printing Company, 1962.

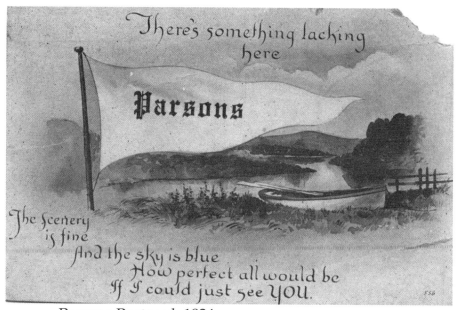

Parsons Postcard, 1924.
Courtesy of Chris Kidwell.

Front row: Franklin and Ruth Mullenax (Mauzy) (Feb. 12, 1931 - May 5, 1987). *Back row*: _____, Foster and Perchie Mullenax (Knotts) (July 9, 1907 - Sept. 5, 1985).
Courtesy of Delain Mullenax.

Parsons postcard, 1917.
Courtesy of Chris Kidwell.

Unknown (World War I soldier could be a Sturms); from Holly Meadows (Etta Sturms), Parsons, postcard.
Courtesy of Chris Kidwell.

Left to right: Bess Kalar Lambert *holding her son* James Kenton Lambert, _____, _____, Dove Kalar Corrick with glasses, J. Blaine Corrick, Mable Kalar Buchanan, *far right*, Parsons, 1911 postcard.
Courtesy of Chris Kidwell.

Tucker County Courthouse, postcard. Sheriff's residence and jail are seen in the middle of the photo.
Courtesy of Chris Kidwell.

Tucker County Courthouse, winter card.
Courtesy of Chris Kidwell.

Parsons postcard, 1909, Tucker County Courthouse.
Courtesy of Chris Kidwell.

Courthouse, Parsons. Sign *on left* reads "Bear Brothers".
Courtesy of Chris Kidwell.

Parsons Courthouse, 1907, and Lloyd Hansford Building postcard.
Courtesy of Chris Kidwell.

13

Peter Pan Cleaners and delivery truck, operated by Jeff Mullennex, 1950s. *Courtesy of Chris Kidwell.*

Second Street, Parsons. *Courtesy of Chris Kidwell.*

2 OND STREET, PARSONS. W.VA   32

First Street, Parsons, postcard. *Courtesy of Chris Kidwell.*

Front Street   Parsons, W.Va.

Miscellaneous Children -- *Courtesy of Shaffer.*

Tucker County Fair event. *Left to right:* Isom Judy and Lloyd Phillips. *Courtesy of Chris Kidwell.*

WALNUT ST. PARSONS, W.VA.

Walnut Street, Parsons, postcard. *Courtesy of Chris Kidwell.*

ELECTION—TUESDAY, NOVEMBER 3, 1936

W. B. MARTIN

REPUBLICAN CANDIDATE FOR

JUSTICE OF THE PEACE

(Black Fork District)

YOUR SUPPORT AND INFLUENCE WILL BE APPRECIATED

Parsons. *Courtesy of Chris Kidwell.*

Jenny Helmick Jenkins,
a nurse at Tucker County Hospital.
Courtesy of Chris Kidwell.

Dale Ashby with his
home in background,
Quality Hill, Loughry
Street.
Courtesy of Chris Kidwell.

Walnut Street, Parsons.
Courtesy of Chris Kidwell.

Elmer and Sylvia Mullenax
with their daughter, Ruth,
Sugarlands.
Courtesy of Delain Mullenax.

Jim's Cozy Corner, Walnut Street, Parsons. J.B. Hulings, owner, postcard.
Courtesy of Chris Kidwell.

J. Russell Hall, caller of the parades at the Tucker County Fair, Second Street, Parsons, passing Plummer Baker's Store; then known as Ford's Store, postcard.
Courtesy of Chris Kidwell.

15

Residence of J.B. Jenkins, former sheriff of Parsons, postcard. Then the location of the Lorren and Irene Bonner Lambert home; now owned by George and Mariwyn McClain Smith.
Courtesy of Chris Kidwell.

The G.L. Elban home, 1909; in the 1970s became the Edward and Lola Plumley home, Pennsylvania Avenue, Parsons, postcard.
Courtesy of Chris Kidwell.

First Street, Parsons, postcard, 1940s.
Courtesy of Chris Kidwell.

Tucker County Bank Building, First Street, Parsons.
Courtesy of Chris Kidwell.

First Street, Parsons,
1910, postcard.
Courtesy of Chris Kidwell.

Walnut Street, Parsons, postcard. Building at center of
photo is Kniceley's Hard-
ware.
Courtesy of Chris Kidwell.

First Street, Parsons, post-
card. Photo taken by Ken
McClain, 1960s.
Courtesy of Chris Kidwell.

Arlington Hotel,
Parsons, postcard.
Courtesy of Chris Kidwell.

17

Western Maryland Railroad Depot, Parsons, postcard.
Courtesy of Chris Kidwell.

Unknown, Parsons,
from Etta Sturms family.
Courtesy of Chris Kidwell.

County and Railroad Bridges, (top of the courthouse
is visible at end of bridge) Parsons, postcard.
Courtesy of Chris Kidwell.

World War II. Jay Moran's
nephew; Frank Moran's son.
Courtesy of Chris Kidwell.

County and railroad bridges, Rt. 219, Parsons, on the main street
through Parsons, postcard. Building on left and bridge are gone; railroad bridge restored in 2011.
Courtesy of Chris Kidwell.

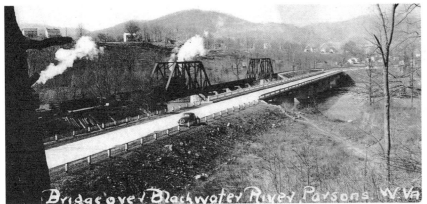

Western Maryland Railroad engines getting a run for Black-water Canyon, 1940s. Billings Avenue can be seen in the background as well as Blackwater Bridge. Parsons.
Courtesy of Chris Kidwell.

Western Maryland Railroad Depot, Parsons, postcard.
Courtesy of Chris Kidwell.

County and Railroad Bridges,
Parsons, postcard.
Courtesy of Chris Kidwell.

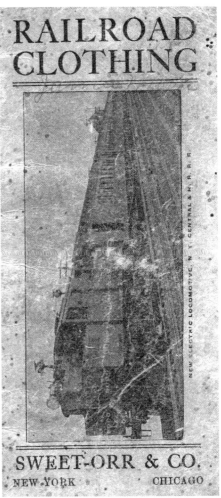

Railroad Clothing booklet, Robinson Brothers (a clothing store in 1907) overalls ad, Parsons.
Courtesy of Chris Kidwell.

Shaver's Fork of Cheat River, Parsons, postcard. Old Ford garage *on the right.*
Courtesy of Chris Kidwell.

Cheat River seen from Route 72 near Parsons, postcard.
Courtesy of Chris Kidwell.

County bridge over Black Fork behind Pennsylvania Avenue, Parsons, postcard; replaced to present site in the 1940s.
Courtesy of Chris Kidwell.

Hoy (or Roy) Ferguson, World War I, France, Parsons; from Holly Meadows (Etta Sturms family photo).
Courtesy of Chris Kidwell.

Unknown, Holly Meadows, Parsons postcard.
From the Etta Sturms Family.
Courtesy of Chris Kidwell.

Unknown, Holly Meadows,
Parsons. From the Etta Sturms Family.
Courtesy of Chris Kidwell.

Workers at the Parsons Tannery circa 1910, Parsons.
Courtesy of Chris Kidwell.

Page Goss Kisner lived in Holly Meadows by the Moss Bridge. He was the father of Richard and James Kisner.
Courtesy of Chris Kidwell.

Unknown, Holly Meadows, Parsons. From the Etta Sturms Family.
Courtesy of Chris Kidwell.

Pulp Mill Addition, Parsons, postcard.
Courtesy of Chris Kidwell.

Sister and brother,
Bertha and Tom Hedrick.
Courtesy of Chris Kidwell.

Pulp Mill Crew,
June 3, 1912, Parsons.
Courtesy of Chris Kidwell.

Pulp Mill crew, Parsons, postcard.
Courtesy of Chris Kidwell.

Lena Nesbit, 1926, hunting, Parsons.
Courtesy of Chris Kidwell.

Courtesy of Chris Kidwell.

Pulp Mill, Parsons, postcard.
Courtesy of Chris Kidwell.

Left to right: Ruth Mullenax,
Patty Goff and Margaret
Ellen Barb, circa 1949.
Courtesy of Kim Michael Wilfong.

Pulp Mill, 1907, Parsons, postcard.
Courtesy of Chris Kidwell.

SCHOOL DAYS

1952-53

Clara "Jill" Wolf, Parsons High School.
Courtesy of Mariwyn McClain Smith.

Pulp Mill, Parsons, postcard.
Courtesy of Chris Kidwell.

Front row, left to right: The Mauzy Family -- Martin, James, Soloman P., Martha, Martha Alice Judy, Edward and Michael; *back row:* Sedgwick, Sally, Catherine, Grace, Elizabeth and Jacob. *Courtesy of Chris Kidwell.*

Pulp Mill, 1912, Parsons, postcard.
Postcard courtesy of Chris Kidwell.

H. S. SHAFFER,
REPUBLICAN NOMINEE FOR
County Superintendent of Schools
Your Support is Solicited.

H.S. Shaffer ad.
Courtesy of Chris Kidwell.

Leecie Mullenax.
Courtesy of Delain Mullenax.

Dam at Shaver's Fork, Parsons, postcard.
Courtesy of Chris Kidwell.

24

Unknown, Parsons. Etta Sturms family,
Holly Meadows.
Courtesy of Chris Kidwell.

Harold L. Barb, Parsons,
born 1894, son of James S.C.
and Mary J. Barb; brother to
Ruben Barb.
Courtesy of Chris Kidwell.

Photo from Clara Rightmire family, Parsons. *Back row, sixth from the left:* Cyrus H. Parsons;
front row, second from the left sitting: Karl Dewey Myers (poet).
Courtesy of Chris Kidwell.

Denzil Lee Judy, born April 2, 1929, the son of Isom and Gertrude Bodkin Judy, killed in Korea by a landmine, May 20, 1951. Buried in Parsons City Cemetery.
Courtesy of Chris Kidwell.

Denver Harness Judy April 1944.
Courtesy of Chris Kidwell.

DEAR GOD

Dear God, I can't pray and say all the things I want at the close of day;
I know you'll be with me, and always will.
But I'll try to pray, till my lips are still.

Dear God, bless my mother so good and true,
For she's been through what I'll never go through.
And now there's a war and I'm far away that's why
I kneel and try to pray.

Dear God, help me keep the vows that I made,
For o'er the sea of troubles are temptations I'll wade.
Give me strength that my mother holds, and her prayers will keep me within her folds.

Dear God bless my father, I'm proud to be his son.
For he is helping us all, so this war can be won.
He's back at the job, and is doing his part,
Putting everything He's got with all his heart.

Dear God bless my "sis", she's so sweet and shy.
We had quarrels, at times she would cry.
I'm sorry, Dear God, for hurting her so.
For she's always in my heart, wherever I go.

Dear God bless my girl, so pretty and sweet.
Guide her and keep her, until again we meet.
May our love stay as strong as when I went away.
Please, Dear God it is so hard to pray.

Dear God, bless my home, were fighting to keep.
Where first I met you at my mother's feet.
My family is there, and all that I own, so please,
Dear God, bless my lovely home.

Dear God, when the war is over and through.
And this proud world vows to do homage to you.
There'll be millions and millions who have come to say:
Dear God, it's just me, I've learned to PRAY.

This poem was composed by Pfc Denver H. Judy, sent

Written by Denver Judy.

"Round Wood Pelers, Parsons, WVa". Unknown workers with the exception of (*left to right*): Number 1 is John Suman Haller, numbers 3 and 4 are Moores, Number 5 is Bob Dawsin and Number 2 *on the far right* is Reasie Auvil.
Courtesy of David and Rita Roberts.

Wade Kidwell eating melon at his home at Jameson Avenue, Parsons.
Courtesy of Chris Kidwell.

Shirley Barton and Bill Judy.
Courtesy of Chris Kidwell.

Nest and Mary Hansford,
Parsons, postcard.
Courtesy of Chris Kidwell.

Mary Wamsley Hansford with her son
Bill Hansford born September 24, 1893.
Courtesy of Chris Kidwell.

Nest Hansford ran a
boardinghouse and Swed-
ish massage parlor in her
home with her sister Mary.
Courtesy of Chris Kidwell.

William Hansford,
lawyer in Tuck-
er County and his
wife Mary Wamsley
Hansford.
Courtesy of Chris Kidwell.

Poling, City Photographer,
PARSONS, WEST VIGINIA

Poling, City Photographer,
PARSONS, WEST VIGINIA

Couple *on the left* are Henry "Mac" Hughes (1860-1926) and Ida F. Hughes (1870-1951). Second couple, Sarah Alice Harsh, (April 22, 1876 - November 16, 1946) and James William Kidwell, (February 7, 1871 - February 3, 1938). They were married May 20, 1896.
Courtesy of Chris Kidwell.

Nest Hazel Hansford and brother, William (Bill) Lamarr Hansford -- children of William and Mary Hansford.
Courtesy of Chris Kidwell.

Della Auvil and Alice Harsh Kidwell. Alice was Della's aunt.
Courtesy of Chris Kidwell.

H.E. McKenzie Jeweler/J.W. Minear Undertaker and General Store, Walnut Street, Parsons.
Courtesy of Jane H. Barb.

Clara Rightmire family, Parsons.
Courtesy of Chris Kidwell.

Clara Rightmire family, Parsons.
Courtesy of Chris Kidwell.

Luther Sturms, Holly Meadows, Parsons.
Courtesy of Chris Kidwell.

Luther William Sturms, Parsons. World War I soldier, (Nov. 17, 1884 - 1970). Registered for the draft Sept. 12, 1918. Buried at Bethel Cemetery, Holly Meadows.
Courtesy of Chris Kidwell.

Clara Rightmire family, Parsons.
Courtesy of Chris Kidwell.

Unknown, Parsons. Etta Sturms family,
Holly Meadows.
Courtesy of Chris Kidwell.

Unknown, Parsons. Etta Sturms family,
Holly Meadows.
Courtesy of Chris Kidwell.

Unknown, Parsons. Etta Sturms family,
Holly Meadows.
Courtesy of Chris Kidwell.

Laura Sturms Flanagan
at Laneville.
Courtesy of Chris Kidwell.

MERRY CHRISTMAS AND A HAPPY NEW YEAR

Lloyd Hansford home, Parsons.
Courtesy of Chris Kidwell.

Carl Miller, Parsons.
Courtesy of Chris Kidwell.

John S. Flanagan, (b. Mar. 23, 1918) Parsons. Corporal in 282 Company 141 Bn. in France. Son of Jacob and Laura Sturms Flanagan, Laneville.
Courtesy of Chris Kidwell.

Unknown, Parsons photo.
From Etta Sturms, Holly Meadows.
Courtesy of Chris Kidwell.

Unknown, Parsons photo.
From Etta Sturms family, Holly Meadows.
Courtesy of Chris Kidwell.

Unknown, Parsons photo.
From Etta Sturms, Holly Meadows.
Courtesy of Chris Kidwell.

Lorean Sturms and sister, daughters of Sam and Emma Sturms, Holly Meadows, Parsons.
Courtesy of Chris Kidwell.

Carl West house, located at the intersection of Slip Hill Road and Sugarlands Road, Parsons.
Courtesy of Chris Kidwell.

Auvil and Parsons General Store, Parsons, 1920s.
Courtesy of Chris Kidwell.

Vemelda Parsons, daughter of Cyrus and Addie Parsons, Holly Meadows, Parsons.
Courtesy of Chris Kidwell.

Delain Bohon, Richard Mauzy and Dorothy Shaffer, Parsons.
Courtesy of Delain Mullenax.

Lorean Sturms, Holly Meadows, daughter of Sam and Emma Sturms. at Whitmer.
Courtesy of Chris Kidwell.

Church group, Parsons, along Cheat River Moss Bridge, Holly Meadows.
Courtesy of Chris Kidwell.

Nest and William Hansford,
Parsons, postcard.
Courtesy of Chris Kidwell.

Leecie and Lillie (Helmick) Mullenax, Parsons.
Courtesy of Delain Mullenax.

Second from left sitting on first step, Sam Sturms, and Parsons
Peeling Crew, Pulp Mill Bottom, Parsons.
Courtesy of Chris Kidwell.

Standing Nick Elza (son of Alfred Elza),
John White, Little Jim Elza, and *seated*
Big Jim Elza.
Courtesy of Chris Kidwell.

Matchbook cover.
Courtesy of Chris Kidwell.

Rosey Lipscomb Antique Shop,
First Street, Parsons, postcard.
Courtesy of Chris Kidwell.

Ed and June Hardy of Porterwood, Pheasant Run. Parents of many children including
Roy, Oscar, Daniel, and Doyle, postcard.
Courtesy of Flossie Hardy.

Paul Holt, Parsons,
World War II.
Courtesy of Chris Kidwell.

Currence Brothers and Clerks, Parsons, postcard.
Courtesy of Jane H. Barb.

Horse Shoeing Wagon & Carriage Repair-
ing, postcard. (Possibly Howard Lipscomb's
Blacksmith Shop.)
Courtesy of Chris Kidwell.

Lloyd Hansford's house, Parsons. Kids sled riding on the hill near First United Methodist Church,
early 1900s.
Courtesy of Chris Kidwell.

Soda fountain at Barb's Drug Store,
Walnut Street, Parsons.
Courtesy of Jane H.Barb.

Main Street, Parsons, courthouse records being brought to Parsons from St. George. Building with scaffolding was office of *The Parsons Advocate* from 1898-2003; now McClain Printing Company.
Courtesy of Jane H. Barb.

Wade Kidwell's ad for his first store across from the First National Bank in the 1940s. He built the building below at 413 First Street, Parsons. The business was sold in 1989.
Courtesy of Chris Kidwell.

The Kidwell family, Parsons.
Left to right: Dick, Carol (holding Chris), David, and Neal.
Courtesy of Chris Kidwell.

Children of James William and Sarah Alice Harsh Kidwell, 1973. *Left to right*: Goldie Snyder, Bess Munson, Louise Rule, Opal Stemple, John Wade Kidwell and Ruth Virginia Hull.
Courtesy of Chris Kidwell.

Sugarlands -- Mullenax reunion, circa 1935: Those pictured include Leecie Mullenax, Elmer Mullenax, Sylvia Knotts Mullenax, Rose Knotts Mullenax, Foster Mullenax, Ruth Mullenax, Frank Mullenax, Lillie Helmick Mullenax, Delton Mullenax, Richard Mullenax, and Lester Mullenax.
Courtesy of Delain Mullenax.

Ruth Mullenax, Elfreda and Luke Mullenax, and Foster Mullenax at the Amigo Cafe, owned by Foster and Ruth's parents Elmer and Sylvia Mullenax, Walnut Street, Parsons.
Courtesy of Delain Mullenax.

1929, Clover Run, home of Samuel and Celia Delaughter. *Front row fourth from the left* Mary C. Harsh; *middle row:* Celia Delaughter, _____, Ellen Harsh, Jay Moran, _____; *back row:* Mae Harsh, Samuel Delaughter and _____.
Courtesy of Chris Kidwell.

Clarence Wilson driving the team, Fork Mountain, Parsons, postcard.
Courtesy of Chris Kidwell.

Mullenax Lumber Company Truck, Parsons.
Courtesy of Delain Mullenax.

Photo from Charleston Newspapers

FDR and friends

MOST presidents find time for West Virginia when election day rolls around. This Oct. 1, 1936, photograph of the unmistakable profile of President Franklin D. Roosevelt taking a tour of Thomas in Tucker County includes four of the most memorable politicians in Mountain State history.

On the left with his hand in his pocket is Jennings Randolph, next FDR and Gov. H. Guy Kump. In the white coat is Sen. Matthew M. Neely and next is the smiling Homer Holt.

It is astonishing to consider that just three years earlier in 1933, the mayor of Chicago, Anton Cermak, was assassinated while riding in a car with President Roosevelt.

Evidence indicated that the president was meant to be the target but Cermak took the five bullets.

Open cars continued to be a standard part of presidential appearances through three decades until that fateful day in Dallas when John Kennedy chose to ride in an open car.

Now, the Secret Service has learned its lesson and presidential cars are heavily armored.

Imagine World War II if President Roosevelt had died that day in 1933.

If President Kennedy had not died in Dallas, would the Vietnam War have turned out differently?

Richard Andre is a local historian and author. His most recent book is "Kanawha Images, Volume Two.

Newspaper clipping from Charleston newspapers of FDR and friends.
Courtesy of Delain Mullenax.

School Picnic, Sugarlands.
Courtesy of Delain Mullenax.

1920s -- Roscoe Arbogast Brothers Garage and Gas Station in the old Ford garage building. Notice the iron railing of the old iron bridge over Shaver's Fork River.
Courtesy of Chris Kidwell.

Samuel and Celia Delaughter, Clover Run. Parents of Cline Delaughter.
Courtesy of Chris Kidwell.

K of P (Knights of Pythias) Hall, Main Street, Parsons, postcard. Used temporarily as the courthouse while the present one was built. Razed in 2007.
Courtesy of Chris Kidwell.

Parsons.
Courtesy of Jane H. Barb.

Horse and buggy crossing bridge.
Courtesy of Jane H. Barb.

Western Maryland Railroad bridge over Black Fork River, Parsons.
Courtesy of Jane H. Barb.

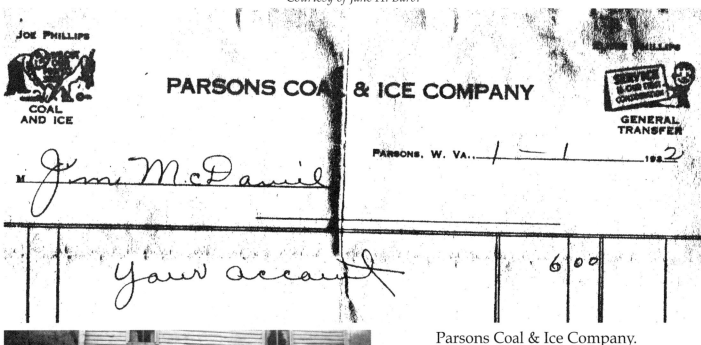

Parsons Coal & Ice Company.
Courtesy of Chris Kidwell.

The Harsh Family, November 10, 1929. *Left to right*: John Harsh, Mary Harsh, _____, Mae Harsh, _____, _____, Ellen Harsh, _____ and Ernest (young boy), Clover Run.
Courtesy of Chris Kidwell.

After the feature of W. F. (Vander) Lipscomb, 90, of Parsons, was carried a few weeks ago, he received a letter from C. J. Maxwell, Fresno, Calif., who will soon be 85. "Vander" brought in the picture above (property of Mrs. Anna Lake of Parsons) thinking that it included a picture of Mr. Maxwell, but after having them all identified, it appears that the only one in the group now living is Mr. Lipscomb. Shown are, standing, left to right—Pud Miller, Dan Ryan, Howard Shaffer, Arch Lipscomb, Bode Stalnaker, Frank Lipscomb, Frank Talbott, Howard Talbott.

Sitting, same order—Joe Minear, Cam Miller, Bruce Minear, Cam Lipscomb, Howard Baker and Creed Minear.

Since Tucker County itself will be 100 years old next year, it seems appropriate at this time to carry the following letter from a native of Tucker County who left here 66 years ago to a native of Preston County who came here and has made his home in Tucker County for more than three quarters of a century.

Mr. Maxwell's letter:
2695 Blackstone Ave.
Fresno, Calif.
Dear "Vander":

by nature and training woodsmen. I well remember your father. That was always his work and he was an excellent, capable man at it. I knew you were a little older than I am but was a little surprised to see how much. Soon I will be 85 but I will never last as long as you have. My heart has about quit functioning and without a heart one can not do much.

It is odd how names cling to a person. My brother Hu called you Vander and I see it has clung to you for over 70 years. I hope you will continue to keep at work on your garden. It is good for you to be out of doors and to have an interest.

Very, very few of the friends of my youth are still alive. I left West Virginia in 1889 and since then have been back only for short visits. The old (St. George) Academy group are mostly gone. But this is a little unusual for the first graduating class at the academy. There were four of us, Addie Adams, Cora Callahan Jared Wamsley and I. Three of us are still on top of the earth; an unusual number.

Sometime when you have time and inclination drop me a line. It will be welcomed.

Tucker Soldier Has Not Filed Claim for Compensation

Michael A. Taylor of Route 2, St. George, is listed among former West Virginia prisoners of war in Korea who have not filed a claim for compensation under Public Law 615, the office of U. S. Senator Harley M. Kilgore has disclosed.

Under the law, former prisoners of war in Korea are entitled to payment of $2.50 a day for each day of imprisonment. The deadline for most such claims is Aug. 21, 1955.

Taylor's number was given as RA 13349296 and a sister, Miss Grace A. Taylor of Route 2, St. George was listed as kin.

In cases of death, the widow, husband, children or parents may file claims.

COURT HOUSE HOURS CHANGE

Ronald L. Hockman, sheriff of Tucker County, has announced that effective July 25 through Sept. 12, the Court House will

Courtesy of Chris Kidwell.

COME IN

will pay that overdue subscription account. Don't wait until the paper stops.

PARSONS ADVOCATE.

PATRONIZE

the merchants who advertise in The Advocate. They will treat you right!

VOLUME XXVII—NO. 8   PARSONS, TUCKER COUNTY, WEST VIRGINIA, THURSDAY, FEBRUARY 22, 1923 $1.50 PER YEAR—IN ADVANCE

THE CARE OF UNFORTUNATES

Child Welfare Commission Presents Plans for Consideration

The creation of homes in each congressional district of the State of West Virginia for the care and support of the poor is one of the new bills proposed by the State Child Welfare Commission which was appointed by Governor Morgan last spring to investigate conditions existing in the state affecting child welfare and to present some program of legislation to be voted upon at the 1923 session of the legislature.

For many months the commission has worked hard and long and finally worked out a program, which if adopted entirely, will place West Virginia among the foremost states in the care of her unfortunates. This program, which was presented for the first time on the last day of the first term of the legislature, contains two bills by way of low legislation, a number of amendments and recommendations regarding old laws and a few enactments of the programs of other commissions. The program will be presented for discussion and vote during the March and April term of the legislature.

In its work the commission sought to avoid any measures which would increase the taxes of the citizens of the state and endeavor to make its program practical and economical as possible. As a result of untiring efforts the members of the child welfare commission have prepared legislation which will

OGDEN ADDS SUTTON PAPER

Herchel C. Ogden, Wheeling newspaper publisher, and G. A. Bolden, Charleston newspaperman, have purchased the newspaper and plant of the Braxton Central, a weekly newspaper published at Sutton, and have taken charge of it. For the present Mr. Bolden will have charge of the editorial department and Mr. Charles M. Bryne, with the newspaper for a number of years will be in charge of the mechanical department. The Central was established 40 years ago by J. H. Dunn, who managed it until a few months prior to his death last November.

Bygone Days

When its very cold some morning,
And the snow is falling too;
The wind is whistling 'round the house,
And you've nothing much to do.

What a time then to be musin',
Of the times that used to be,
When you were a little shaver,
And sat at your mothers knee.

With her hand upon your forehead,
And her arm about you entwined;
Listening to her stories
With all your heart and mind.

As she tells of the days of her girlhood,
With war and sorrow untold,
With sheep skins, rebels and red men,
And your heart begins to grow bold.

Well, you long for the time of

Preachers Entertained

Last Friday Mrs. J. B. Corrick and Mrs. C. W. Minear gave a dinner to the ministers and helpers, at Mrs. Corrick's home.

Nine ministers were present and after a most delicious dinner, an hour was spent in social conversation, singing of old favorite songs, and prayer. The guests then departed voting their thanks to the hostesses and acknowledging a first class time.

VALUE OF SILAGE TO FATTEN BEEF CATTLE

Two-Year-Old Steers Prove to Be Most Satisfactory.

Feeding Linseed Meal and Clover or Alfalfa in Addition is Recommended—Full Feeding of Corn is Not Favored.

Experimental work by the University of Missouri College of Agriculture has shown—

That highly satisfactory beef can be produced from two-year-old steers by feeding the corn as silage, together with linseed meal and clover or alfalfa hay, instead of full feeding on shelled or ear corn.

That the price of feed and the premium on heavily fed cattle during the past five years has not warranted full feeding over long periods, when cattle which are two years or more of age are used.

That one acre, yielding 40 bushels of corn, or eight tons of silage, if fed as silage, together with 1,733 pounds of linseed oil meal and 1,810 pounds

Public Sale

I will offer for sale the following personal property, at my residence at the mouth of Maxwell Run on Horse Shoe, on

Saturday, March 3, 1923,
sale beginning at 9 o'clock.

One gray horse, four milch cows, one fresh Jersey cow and three, that will be fresh in March and April, two white O. I. C. hogs, forty-four chickens, one Smith & Barnes piano, one sideboard, one dresser, one sewing machine, one kitchen cabinet, three iron bedsteads, one No. 1 Burnside heating stove, two sets work harness, one hill-side plow, one shovel plow, one light two-horse wagon, one lot of potatoes, one lot of corn, one lot of meat and store goods, and groceries, shoes, sleds and farming tools too tedious to mention. Terms of sale made known on day of sale.

MRS. CHAS. BARR.

Parkersburg Hi Lads Can't Go

MRS. JOHN HEBB PASSES AWAY

Mrs. Martha Hebb, wife of John C. Hebb, of this city, passed to the Great Beyond, Tuesday, after a lingering illness of the past several months from complications incident to her advanced years. At the time of her death Mrs. Hebb was 71 years, 3 months and 21 days old. Deceased was a very kind old lady and the mother of several children. She was also a first cousin of our townsman, W. F. Lipscomb. She was a true christian and since early girlhood days had been a member of the church. She was a loving mother and wife and a true friend and neighbor.

Funeral services and interment will take place at Macedonia tomorrow, the place of her early days, besides those gone on before.

INACCURATE RECORDS KEPT

Charleston—Failure on the part of attendants at births and those handling the dead, to make the proper record of them with the state, has put West Virginia on the black list with the U. S. government. West Virginia is one of two states east of the Mississippi whose birth records are so inaccurate that the U. S. government will not recognize them, is information given out by Dr. Carl E. Raver, director of bureau of vital statistics.

Law requires every child whether born dead or alive, to be registered with the state. Every county has several registrars, and the vital statistics urges the citizens of West Virginia to learn who their registrars are, and cooperate with them. Reputable doctors are particular to attend to their registration, but the bureau states there is gross neglect by attendants where no doctor is employed.

"Death certificates are equally important," says Dr. Raver, "and persons present at time of death should insist upon an immediate filing of death certificate with the state, if they would avoid suspicion and perhaps prosecution. Undertakers should and usually do, attend to this certificate, but there are large areas in West Virginia where no undertakers are available. In these cases, persons handling the corps are responsi-

CHURCH ANNOUNCEMENTS

M. E. Church

Evangelistic services are now in progress. Services every evening at 7:30.

Rev. R. H. Clark, of Thomas, will preach on Saturday evening and on Sunday at 11 a. m. Everybody invited.

—J. W. Bedford, Pastor.

M. E. Church, South

Sunday School 10 a. m. H. W. Auvil, Supt.
Prayer meeting Wednesday evening 7:30 o'clock.
Preaching by the pastor on first and third Sundays of each month at 11 a. m., and every Sunday evening.

DEATH VISITS HARSH HOME

The death angel visited the home of Mr. and Mrs. Aldine Harsh, Monday, and claimed the infant daughter, Mary Francis, aged three months and nine days.

The little tot was taken ill with indigestion and passed out within a few hours. Funeral services were conducted at the home Wednesday afternoon and interment was made in the city cemetery.

HIGH SCHOOL STARTS PAPER

To the Friends of Black Fork District High School.

We are again publishing our High School paper, "The Echo." There is quite a bit of expense connected with the issuing of this paper. Every High School around here has a paper of some kind, and we decided we did not want to be behind in anything so we started a paper which will continue for years and years. Parsons High will be known all over the state by "The Echo."

We have a High School here that every citizen of Black Fork District should feel proud of. The editorial staff nor the student body does not have the money to pay the expenses of running the paper. The paper will be published every month from now until the close of the school term. The subscription

Head of a Purebred Hereford Heifer.

Parsons Advocate front page, 1923.
Courtesy of Delain Mullenax.

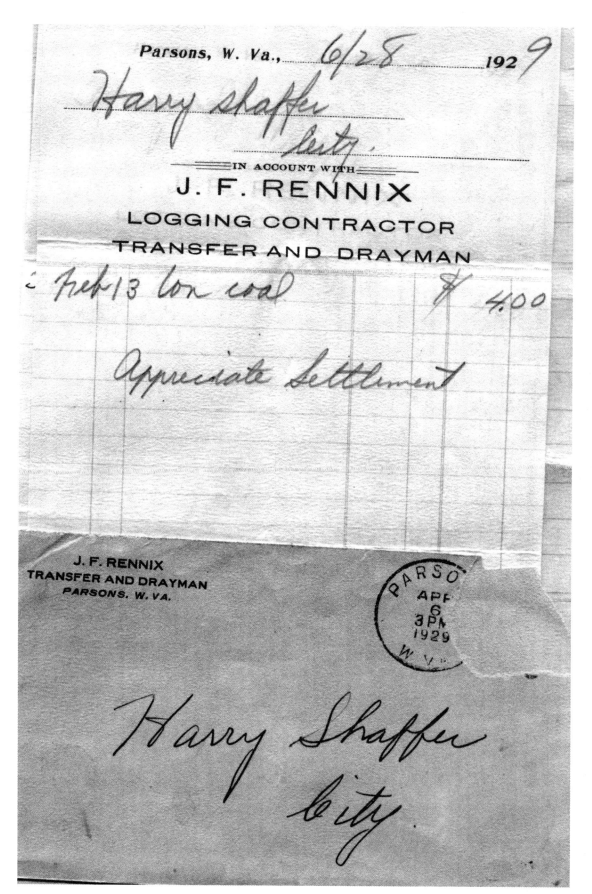

J.F. Rennix Logging Contractor Transfer and Drayman invoice, 1929.
Courtesy of Chris Kidwell.

BLACKMAN'S HARDWARE & FURNITURE
J. F. BLACKMAN, Prop'r
BUILDERS' SUPPLIES   FARMING IMPLEMENTS
PIANOS, VICTROLAS, EDISON PHONOGRAPHS
TERMS 30 DAYS

Parsons, W. Va., 10-27 1925

M _H S Shoffer_

No. _____
MC CASKEY ALLIANCE O

Reg. No.	Clerk P	Account Forwarded	8	52
1	By 1-4in Tile Pits			34
2	By Bar		8	18
3				
4				
5	Rec'd Payment			
6				
7	Oct 31/25			
8				
9	B. Hehr & Fugate			
10	N R			
11				
12				
13				
14				
15				
16				

BLACKMAN'S HARDWARE & FURNITURE
J. F. BLACKMAN, Prop'r
BUILDERS' SUPPLIES   FARMING IMPLEMENTS
PIANOS, VICTROLAS, EDISON PHONOGRAPHS
TERMS 30 DAYS

Parsons, W. Va., 7/30 1925

M _H S Shoffer_

No. _____
MC CASKEY ALLIANCE O

Reg. No.	Clerk P	Account Forwarded		
1	Bolt Lamp	1	50	
2	Cement		10	
3				
4			1	60
5				
6	Pea		50	
7	2 Butty		20	
8	Coal Oven		40	1 10
9				2 70
10	By P			50
11				1 20
12				
13	Paid			
14				
15				
16				

Blackman's Hardware and Furniture Invoice.
Courtesy of Chris Kidwell.

Marsh's Service Station, Parsons.
Courtesy of Jane H. Barb.

E. L. COMBS
PLUMBING, TINNING, PAINTING
WALL PAPER

Parsons, W. Va., _____ 192__

Name _Harry Shaffer_

Address _____

Sold by _____ Am't Rec'd _____

Bibb	3	50
Labor		75
	4	25
Paid		
E. L. Combs		

E. L. COMBS
PLUMBING, TINNING, PAINTING
WALL PAPER

Parsons, W. Va., _10-27_ 192__

Name _H. B._

Address _____

Sold by _____ Am't Rec'd _____

Galvanizing		50
Foot Valve		85
Pipe	3	78
	5	13
Paid		
E. L. Combs		

E.L. Combs Plumbing, Tinning, Painting and Wallpaper, Parsons.
Courtesy of Chris Kidwell.

Ed Combs, Parsons.

The Old Parsons Saw Mill & Grist Mill.
Courtesy of Chris Kidwell.

In 1844, Abraham Parsons (the grandfather of Mrs. Stella Parsons Brown) built on the slough between the two forks of Cheat River in the city of Parsons, at a location believed to have been back of the Fank-houser Handle Factory. The factory was a water-powered saw mill and grist mill which was destroyed by a flood in 1857. This mill was rebuilt in 1859 and sold by Abraham Parsons in 1872 to Abraham Currence.

Rennix Grocery Order Form.
Courtesy of Chris Kidwell.

Left to Right: Joe and Mollie Thornburg, Clara and Silias Irons, ___, Lucy, Henry and Mabel Irons. Photo taken at Granpa Irons's homeplace in Pheasant Run where Uncle Henry lived. Joe and Mollie are Ethel's father and mother-in-law. They lived with Uncle Henry, 1932.
Courtesy of Chris Kidwell.

John and Mary C. Harsh, Clover Run.
Courtesy of Chris Kidwell.

Auvil and Parsons ad 1923, The *Parsons Advocate.*
Courtesy of Chris Kidwell.

Rev. Joseph (minister at St. Johns Methodist Church, 1959-1962) and wife, Goldie.
Courtesy of Chris Kidwell.

Left to right: Roberta Cosner (Dye), Frances Close (Hovatter) and Patricia Goff (Michael).
Courtesy of Kim Michael Wilfong.

Unknown, World War II photo.
Courtesy of Chris Kidwell.

Mike Mauzy, son of Paul and Ruth Mullenax Mauzy.
Courtesy of Delain Mullenax.

Left to right: Kim Michael (Wilfong), Peter S. and James "Chris" Michael.
Courtesy of Kim Michael Wilfong.

Corrick Furniture & Hardware Co. ad, 1923.
The *Parsons Advocate.*
Courtesy of Chris Kidwell.

Left to right: Pat, Chris and Jim Michael,
November 17, 1958.
Courtesy of Kim Michael Wilfong.

Left to right: Patricia Goff (Michael), Roberta Cosner (Dye) and Frances Close (Hovatter).
Courtesy of Kim Michael Wilfong.

Sun Brothers Show, Parsons, 7-21-1909, postcard.
Courtesy of Chris Kidwell.

Left to right: Lorren "Pooch" Lambert and Phillip Harper, Parsons.

Mose Callahan, postcard. A fixture on the Dry Fork Railroad.
Courtesy of Jane H. Barb.

Citizens' Band, Parsons, *left to right front row*: Randy _____, _____, Frank_____, Bill _____, Harry Colebank. *Back row*: _____, Delbert Gilmore, Dewey Repair, Winnie Price, Oney Sturms, Delbert Arbogast, Vernon Squires, _____, _____, _____, Sam Shaffer, postcard.
Courtesy of Chris Kidwell.

"Smittie's Kids," 1911 postcard, Parsons.
Courtesy of Chris Kidwell.

Tucker County Hospital between Main and Chestnut streets, Parsons.
Courtesy of Kim Michael Wilfong.

PROSPECTUS

OF THE

Philippi Blanket Mills

(Incorporated)

PHILIPPI, WEST VIRGINIA

SUBMITTED TO

The Parsons Board of Trade

AND

The Individual Members Thereof

BY

THE PHILIPPI BLANKET MILLS, Inc.

PHILIPPI WEST VIRGINIA

Copy of Terms of Stock Certificate

PAR VALUE $100 PER SHARE

The holder of the Preferred Stock represented by this Certificate is entitled to an Annual Dividend of Ten Percent (10%), payable out of the net profits of the Company before any dividend is paid upon the Common Stock. Should the net profits in any year be insufficient to pay said dividend, either in whole or in part, any unpaid portion thereof shall become a charge against the net profits of the Company, and shall be paid in full out of said net profits before any dividends are paid upon the Common Stock.

In the event of the dissolution of the corporation from any cause, holders of Preferred Stock shall be paid out of the assets to the par value of the stock together with accrued dividends before anything is paid to the holders of the Common Stock. The Preferred Stock shall be subject to redemption at the option of the Company at $105.00 per share any time after five years from date of issue.

Preferred stockholders shall not be entitled to voting privileges, nor to participate in profits beyond its fixed, preferential, cumulative, annual dividend of ten per cent.

nothing in above stock certificate in regard to term same

53

Philippi Blanket Mill, Parsons.
Courtesy of Chris Kidwell.

Philippi Blanket Factory, Parsons.
Courtesy of Chris Kidwell.

Parsons Pulp & Lumber Plant, Parsons.
Courtesy of Jane H. Barb.

Odd Fellows, Parsons.
Courtesy of Jane H. Barb.

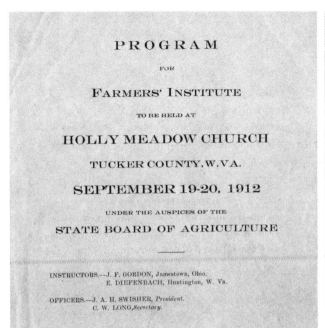

Courtesy of Chris Kidwell.

Howard and Summa Haller at their Esso Station on Route 219, Parsons. The automobile is a Volkswagon Carmegia brought home from Germany by the Haller's son, Dempsey.
Courtesy of David and Rita Roberts.

Haller's Station

Howard Haller's Esso Station on Route 219, Parsons.
Courtesy of David and Rita Roberts.

Unknown World War II soldiers.
Courtesy of Chris Kidwell.

Howard Higgs, 1896, Parsons.
Courtesy of Chris Kidwell.

K. M. POLING,

Artistic ∴ Photographer,

PARSONS, W. VA.

born

Howard Higgs b. 1896

Instantaneous Process Exclusively

Headquarters for the finest crayon, India
ink, water color and oil enlarge-
ments. Also, views of landscape
sceneries. All calls for work
of this kind promptly
attended too.

NOTICE.—The negative of this photograph
is preserved and kept for future
orders. at reduced price.

K.M. Poling, Artistic Photographer, Parsons.
Courtesy of Chris Kidwell.

Foster Mullenax,
July 17, 1927 - July 18, 2005.
Courtesy of Delain Mullenax.

Mabel Knotts Evans, 2001.
Courtesy of Delain Mullenax.

Gary Hovatter, Democrat
for Sheriff ad, Parsons.
Courtesy of Chris Kidwell.

Poling, ⚬°⚬°⚬° Parsons, West Va.

George W. Higgs and Jennie May Dasher Higgs,
married Sept. 19, 1893, Parsons.
Courtesy of Chris Kidwell.

Herbert A. "Dad" Price of
Clover Run, married Mary
A. Varner Price in 1895. They
were the parents of Myrtle,
Delbert F., Mattie B., Varner
Walter, Evert J., Ona V., and
Ernest L. Mr. Price had two
thumbs on one hand and
would put a penny between
them and dare the neighbor-
hood kids to get the penny.
Courtesy of Chris Kidwell.

Sister of the Swish pin for Tucker County Centennial
1856-1956. The women wore this pin. The men wore
the one *at the right*. The men grew beards in recogni-
tion of the event.
Courtesy of Chris Kidwell.

Gwen Mullenax Gilbert.
Courtesy of Delain Mullenax.

*Front row left to right:*_____ Baker, Rhelda Knotts, Verda Knotts, _____ White, and _____. *Back row left to righ*t: Jackie Jones, Betty Knotts, Delain Bohon, Carol Hebb and Beulah Lipscomb, 1944.
Courtesy of Delain Mullenax.

CCC Certificate of Discharge, 1934,
from the War Department.

Blackfork District High School; Parsons High School, Parsons; later Parsons Graded School, corner of Second and Chestnut streets, postcard.
Courtesy of Chris Kidwell.

Mr. Harry Stalnaker Shaffer, teacher.
Courtesy of Shaffer.

Delton Mullenax,
1949-1950.
Courtesy of Delain Mullenax.

Dewight's Auto Repair, (located next to Kidwell Auto Parts) Dewight Bright, August 1980.
Courtesy of Chris Kidwell.

Mariwyn McClain (Smith), Dixie Goff (Gutmann) and Phyllis Donalds (Nairn). Parsons High School Class of 1955.
Courtesy of Madonna DiBacco.

Carol Jean Kidwell (Mar. 5, 1939-Aug. 1, 1993) modeling in Washington, DC, 1960s.
Courtesy of Chris Kidwell.

Old Farmer's Inn between Parsons and Elkins. Sign reads "Open -- Cold Beer".
Courtesy of Chris Kidwell.

Joyce Hebb and Kenny Tabler, April 25, 1948.
Courtesy of Delain Mullenax.

Mullenax Lumber Company, owned by Elmer Mullenax.
Courtesy of Delain Mullenax.

Porterwood Lumber Co., Porterwood, 1913-1927. Owned by Wilson Lumber Company.
Courtesy of Chris Kidwell.

Debbie Daughtery and
Neal Kidwell, Quality Hill.
Courtesy of Chris Kidwell.

Earl Corcoran
with his hunt-
ed rattlesnakes
with Rock and
Rick Corcoran
(grandchil-
dren), Quality
Hill, August
1965.
*Courtesy of
Chris Kidwell.*

Accounting Letter from Job Parsons, Jr., 1895.
Courtesy of Chris Kidwell.

Corporal Hugh Whis-
man, Hq. Co. 3 Bn. 301
Apo 94, Camp McCain,
Mississippi.
Courtesy of Chris Kidwell.

Freight wreck, Parsons, 1907, postcard.
Courtesy of Chris Kidwell.

World War II, Corporal E.J. Getz,
Pheasant Run.
Courtesy of Chris Kidwell.

Doyle Hardy,
World War II, Parsons.
Courtesy of Chris Kidwell.

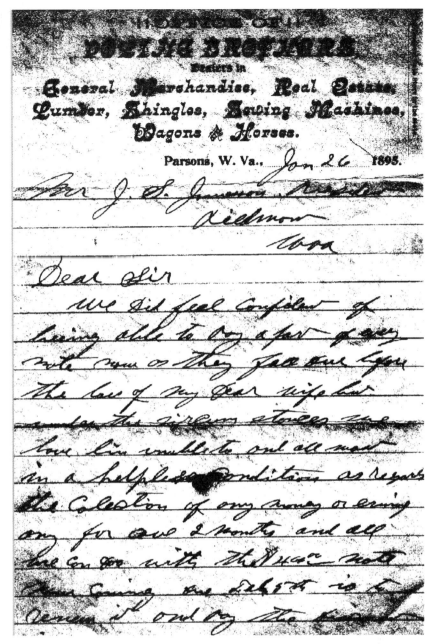

Poling Brothers letterhead 1895.
Courtesy of Chris Kidwell.

Parsons Civil Conservation Corps Camp,
November 22, 1953.
Courtesy of Chris Kidwell.

Bert Price's carport -- pet deer, "Poncho,"
Leah Marco standing, 1976.
Courtesy of Chris Kidwell.

Homer Floyd Fansler's family. He is holding his son Gerald Lee Verne Fansler. *Seated to his right* is Stephen Truman Fansler, photographer in Thomas from 1892 to 1910.
Courtesy of Jane H. Barb.

Ellis Barnes and wife with Pitt Bull in Parsons. Courthouse in background.
Courtesy of Chris Kidwell.

First Street in Parsons in 1889

Shaver's Fork Railroad bridge is *in the center*, Turkey Knob is *on the right*, the Tucker County Bank was built where the tent is located.
Courtesy of Chris Kidwell.

Stanley A. and Elizabeth Minear Hehle were married by Rev. R.O. Lucke in August 1929. They were the parents of Mary Josephine (Mrs. William) Jones and Elizabeth Jean (Mrs. Michael) Ledden.
Courtesy of Mariwyn McClain Smith.

It You Can't Laugh Don't Come To See
THE
"WOMANLESS WEDDING"
NOVEMBER 18 & 19

SPONSORED BY THE RIVER CITY CLUB, TO BE PRESENTED AT THE VICTORIA THEATRE, NOV. 18, AND HIGH SCHOOL AUDITORIUM, NOV. 19, PARSONS, W. VA., by SYMPSON LEVIE COMPANY, OF BARDSTOWN, KENTUCKY

80   LOCAL MEN AS CHARACTERS   80
Biggest Affair Ever Staged in Parsons
SCREAMS OF LAUGHTER   BE SURE TO
COME

ALL STAR CAST

All Star Cast headed by C. W. Minear as leading lady.
Butler _____ P. L. Marsh
Punch Girls _____ Frank Swink and Jule Cross
Present Takers _____ Sylvanus Harper and D. C. Rennix
Mother _____ W. K. Pritt
Father _____ R. V. Willson
Little Brothers _____ Ralph Horne and J. F. Dumire
Ikey _____ Claude Bailey
Old Maid _____ B. W. Post
Grandmother _____ H. A. Ridgway
Grandfather _____ Geo. H. Wolfe
Charlie Chaplin _____ Eddie Lipscomb
Uncle from Clover Run ____ Fred Combs
Aunt from Clover Run ____ C. W. Harvey
Twin Sisters ____ A. P. and Jake Bennett
Mary Pickford _____ Chas. Roberts, Jr.
Fritz Kreisler _____ E. N. Phillips
Groom's Uncle _____ J. F. Robinson
Groom's Aunt _____ C. R. Parsons
Haughty Mother _____ B. E. Kimble
Haughty Father _____ R. O. Lucke
The Fashion Plate _____ Leonard Ours
Harry Lauder _____ R. H. Anderson
Thos. A. Edison _____ S. M. Kendall
Mrs. Edison _____ J. E. Poling
Country Cousin _____ H. G. Johnson, Jr.
Pat O'Grady _____ Harold Felton
Rosie O'Grady _____ C. G. Shaffer
Annie Laurie _____ Willard Pritt
Hen-Pecked Huband _____ Mike Hill
Devoted Wife __ Otis (Shang) Phillips
Flapper _____ Kent Lambert
President Hoover _____ C. A. Roberts
Mrs. Hoover _____ Chas. Buchanan
Negro Mammy _____ Lewis Spangler

The Baby _____ D. W. Thurston
J. Gould _____ O. G. Hovatter
Mrs. Gould _____ G. W. Kelley
Ex-Pres. Coolidge ___ W. E. Whiteside
Mrs. Coolidge _____ John McNeeley
Kentucky Colonel ____ W. F. Randolph
His Lady _____ Bascom Parsons
Village School Marm Herman Lambert
Mr. Vanderbilt _____ E. C. Sine
Mrs. Vanderbilt _____ B. D. Carter
General Pershing __ A. Brooke Withers
Col. Charles Lindberg ____ Ray Jenkins
Theda Bara _____ Homan Hall
John D. Rockefeller _____ S. S. Ford
Mrs. Rockefeller _____ A. D. Strader
Henry Ford _____ H. D. Wilfong
Mrs. Henry Ford _____ C. D. Sturms
Madam Schumann Heink _____ F. Elwood Baker
— The Wedding Party —
Groomsmen — Clarence Fankhauser, R. H. O'Haver, D. F. Collins, Slate Poitevint, W. W. Myers , Edgar Combs
Pages ____ John Auvil, Bud Lipscomb
Bishop _____ G. G. Lambert
Best Man _____ W. T. Taylor
Bridesmaids ____ Tracy Nestor, Kenneth Minear, Gay Nestor, Bus Gatrelle, Mr. Gainer, Ray Long June Collett
Maid of Honor _____ John Long
Matron of Honor _____ Fred Long
Ring Bearer _____ C. O. Headlee
Flower Girls _____ A. B. Simpson and P. W. Smith
Bride _____ C. W. Minear
Groom _____ (?) Guess Who
Train Bearer _____ W. J. Corrick

Newspaper story for play, Parsons.
Courtesy of Jane H. Barb.

Victoria Theatre, November 18-19, 1929.
Courtesy of Phyllis Carr.

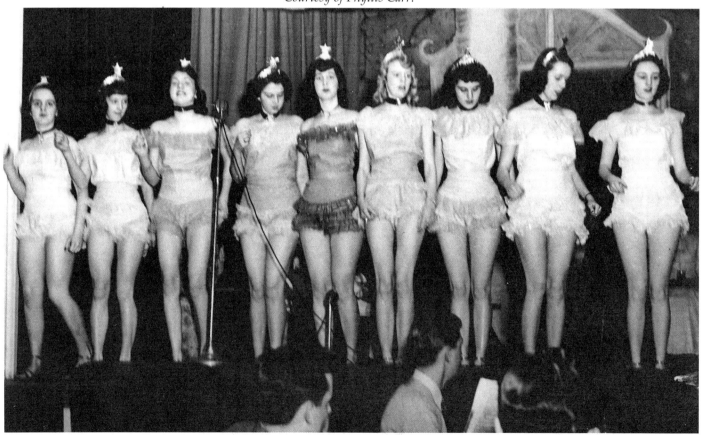

Minstrel Show at Parsons High School -- *left to right:* Judy Gable White, Nancy Barb, Jane Hamrick (Barb), Ruth Mullenax (Mauzy), Deloris Reel, Patty Goff (Michael), Nancy Donalds, Nancy Auvil, and Sally English (George), 1949.
Courtesy of Jane H. Barb.

Minstrel Show at Parsons High School. Joe Bundy, Casey Jones, Deloris Hinebaugh, Bob Barton, Jane Hamrick (Barb), Nancy Donalds, Judy Gable, Cecil Stalnaker, ___, Deloris Reel, Mary McVicker, Ted Dorman, Fred Long, Sally English, Paul Bell, J. Kenton Lambert, Emma Smith, Faith McClain, Elizabeth Bennett, Russ Carr, Bill Minear, ___, ___, Elliott "Fats" Ryan, Frank Ours.
Courtesy of Jane H. Barb.

Hansford Gasoline Station. Current site of Rite Aid and Shop 'N Save in Parsons.
Courtesy of Jane H. Barb.

Mary Hansford Warner with brother, Bill Hansford.
Courtesy of Jane H. Barb.

Hansford Gasoline Station.
Courtesy of Jane H. Barb.

Forty-three bikers attempt the seven-mile hike from Parsons to Hendricks, April 5, 1972. *Left ro right:* Dave Snyder, Mike Bright, Paul Pritt, Mark Bright, Boyd Bosserman, _____, John Connell, Mike Bohon, O.J. Hovatter, Rocky Shahan, Chris Kidwell, _____, Wonda Connell, Robin Plum, Debbie Moore, _____. Remaining participants are unidentified. From The *Parsons Advocate.*
Courtesy of Chris Kidwell.

An early home in Parsons around 1895. Photo taken by J.P. Maxwell, photographer and relative of Hu Maxwell, historian and author.
Courtesy of Chris Kidwell.

Swinging bridge, (Mill Street to Quality Hill) Parsons.
Courtesy of Jane H. Barb.

Lovers' Lane, (sidewalk removed in 2010-2011) U.S. Rt. 219, Parsons.
Courtesy of Jane H. Barb.

View of Parsons, looking west.
Courtesy of Jane H. Barb.

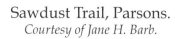

Moss Ford Bridge, postcard, Parsons.
Courtesy of Jane H. Barb.

Sawdust Trail, Parsons.
Courtesy of Jane H. Barb.

Men entering World War II.

Photo taken on top of old Parsons High School (Parsons Graded School), Parsons.
Courtesy of Chris Kidwell.

Boober and Bible Store, Parsons, postcard. (Broadwater postcards in a rack on the counter.)
Courtesy of Chris Kidwell.

Presentation Ceremony

Army-Navy "E" Star
Award

★ ★ ★ ★

Dorman Mills

Parsons, West Virginia

July Twenty-Ninth
Nineteen Hundred Forty-Four
Two o'Clock

Parsons Cemetery, postcard.
Courtesy of Chris Kidwell.

Hobson School children, Texas Mountain, Parsons.

Edward F. McClain, (1935-1995), Parsons High School, Class of 1953.
Courtesy of Mariwyn McClain Smith.

"The Victoria Opera House, Parsons, W.Va.," Walnut and Third streets; later Victoria movie theatre, postcard.
Courtesy of Chris Kidwell.

Ticket for the Victoria Theatre, Parsons.
Courtesy of Chris Kidwell.

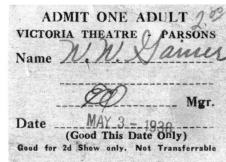

Seneca Trail on the Cheat River near Parsons and Elkins, postcard, 1931.
Courtesy of Chris Kidwell.

Mill Race, Parsons postcard.
Courtesy of Chris Kidwell.

Carl's Motel and Restaurant, Parsons postcard.
Courtesy of Chris Kidwell.

SWARTZ SERVICE STATION
500 FIRST STREET, PARSONS, WEST VIRGINIA, TEL. 42
Studebaker Cuts Your Hauling Costs

Swartz Service Station ad, Parsons.
Courtesy of Chris Kidwell.

Kidwell Auto Parts -- John Wade Kidwell, early 1950s with Isom Judy.
Courtesy of Chris Kidwell.

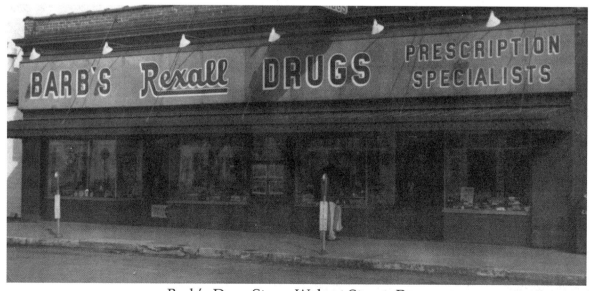

Barb's Drug Store, Walnut Street, Parsons.
Courtesy of Chris Kidwell.

Parsons Volunteer Fire Department fire wagon and Parsons Depot.
Courtesy of Parsons Volunteer Fire Department.

The Parsons Volunteer Fire Department was organized in May 1932. M.M. "Pap" Swearingen was the first motorized fire chief and served in that capacity until 1941.

M.M. "Pap" Swearingen.
*Courtesy of Parsons
Volunteer Fire Department.*

Large fire, Main Street, Parsons, May 21, 1932.
Fawley Building burned.
Courtesy of Parsons Volunteer Fire Department.

June 10, 1944.
Courtesy of Parsons Volunteer Fire Department.

Earl Corcoran.
*Courtesy of Parsons
Volunteer Fire Department.*

PROGRAMME

Parsons Fire Dept. Minstrel

VICTORIA THEATRE

FRIDAY, MARCH 31, 1933

Given Under the Auspices and for Benefit of

The Parsons Fire Department

C. W. FISHER, DIRECTOR

60 Clean, Entertaining, Fun-making, Side-
Splitting People 60

*Courtesy of Parsons Volunteer
Fire Department.*

Seventh Annual
Fire School Banquet
*Men's Residence Hall
Wednesday, July 28, 1937*
49 *at 6:30 P. M. sharp
Assessment $1.00* (U. S. Tax Free)

*Courtesy of Parsons
Volunteer Fire Department.*

Parsons Volunteer Firemen who attended the firefighters' tournament at Soldiers' Field in Chicago, September 5, 1937. *Left to right, standing*: Kenneth Stevens, Henry Clair and Bill Bennett; *seated*: Milford (Cooney) Parsons, Earl Corcoran and Darl Stalnaker.
Courtesy of Parsons Volunteer Fire Department.

Darl Stalnaker, past chief of PVFD with Jack Mullenax at PVFD Homecoming Parade, Parsons, circa 1988.
Courtesy of Parsons Volunteer Fire Department.

Parsons's first fire department, January 26, 1933. *Left to right:* Ralph Horne, tannery horse, James Schoonover, driver, Carlton Hehle, Ford Combs, William Gilmore, Howard Vannoy, Chief McKinley Swearingen, Blaine Stokes, William Gatrelle, Carl Powers, Howard Loughry, Edgar Combs, foreman, Winfred Murphy, Hoyt Nestor, Lerah Springer, _____, Earl Corcoron, captain. *Back row left to right:* R. Sheets, R. Digman, G. Vannoy, J. Schoonover, B. Bennett, Lejoy Flanagan. Picture taken by fireman Robert Shrout.
Courtesy of Parsons Volunteer Fire Department.

Parsons Volunteer Fire Department, Parsons, 1938.
Courtesy of Parsons Volunteer Fire Department.

Courtesy of Parsons Volunteer Fire Department.

Minear's Livery Stable Fire, October 12, 1936.
Courtesy of Parsons Volunteer Fire Department.

Moose Building (owned by Leo Goss) fire, September 1983, during the Tucker County Fair, Parsons. Two people who lived upstairs over the Moose Building perished during the fire.
Courtesy of Chris Kidwell.

Granville Good at Fire Hall, Parsons, postcard.
Courtesy of Chris Kidwell.

Parsons Volunteer Fire Department Band.
Courtesy of Parsons Volunteer Fire Department.

Front row left to right: E. Arbogast, B. Pase, B. Norman, and J. Sherman; *back row left to right:* D. Pine, J. Kenny, W. Caldwell, O. Moore, E. Phillips, H. Fox, A. Radcliff and D. Stalnaker.
Courtesy of Parsons Volunteer Fire Department.

Courtesy of Parsons Volunteer Fire Department.

Front row: Casper Bonner, Ben Thompson, Leo Harper, Ray Adams (US Forest Service) and Frank Canfield; *middle row*: Charles (Chuck) Saboites, ____ Harsh, Red Cooper and Darl Stalnaker; *back row:* Frank Roberts, John Knutti, Pete Filler, Lewis Carr, Ernest (Pete) Olson, and Jack Godden (ranger).
Courtesy of Parsons Volunteer Fire Department.

Allen Judy, Darl Stalnaker and Charles Lloyd, 1975.
Courtesy of Parsons Volunteer Fire Department.

Left to right: John Bright, Kenton Lambert, John Prosserc and Darl Stalnaker.
Courtesy of Parsons Volunteer Fire Department.

Parsons Volunteer Fire Department, 1963. *Front row left to right*: Larry Price, Robert N. Pase, Sr. J. Darl Stalnaker, Willard Caldwell, Keith Vance, William "Bill" Harlow, Denny Fink. *Standing*: Charles Rhodes, Kenneth Flynn, Bernard Martin, Robert Shrout (trustee), Luther Bennett (trustee), Hubert Lake (trustee), Paul Fansler, Edward Phillips, Jerry Parsons, Alan "Red" Martin. Trucks: 1956 American LaFrance custom 750 gpm pumper; 1963 Ford F800 American LaFrance 750 gpm pumper.
Courtesy of Parsons Volunteer Fire Department.

The Parsons Advocate's Volunteer Dinner, *first row:* Verl Davis, Bob Pase, Pearl Faye Pase, Bernie Martin, chief, Darl Stalnaker and Ron Sheets; *second row*: Hank Thompson, John Thompson, Dennis Pine, Jim Propst, Fred Trader, Kenny Poling, J. Phillips and Mike Matlick; *third row*: Ernie Carr, Darl James, Kevin White, Ralph Helmick, Larry Price, Charles Lloyd and Neil Auvil; *fourth row*: Phil Phillips, Jack Mullenax, Mark Martin and Charlie Trader.
Courtesy of Parsons Volunteer Fire Department.

Parsons Volunteer Fire Department--late 1970s. *Front row, left to right:* Ernest Carr, John Thompson, Sr., Charles "Frog" Lloyd, Bernard Martin, chief, Preston Simmons, Neil Auvil, Charles "Chuck" Dumire, Jim Blosser. *Standing, left to right:* S. Craig Wilfong, Sr., James N. Propst, Larry Price, James "Jimmy" Propst, John Campbell, J. Darl Stalnaker, Samuel Blosser, Verl "Nubby" Davis, Rusty Shahan, Harold Buchannon, Ronald Sheets, Robert N. Pase, Sr., and Hancel "Hank" Thompson.
Courtesy of Parsons Volunteer Fire Department.

December 15, 1991, Christmas Party. *First row, left to right*: N. Auvil, sec., D. Stalnaker, right chief, C. Lloyd, assistant chief, L. Price, captain, B.R. Martin, chief, C. Wilfong, chaplain, K. White, lieutenant, V. Davis, J. Propst, assistant chief; *second row*: R. Helmick, C. Lantz, D. Wagner, C. Bates, J. Mullenax, lieutenant, D. Nestor, J.D. Alkire, lieutenant, D. Channel; *third row*: R. Mullenax, M. Martin, H. Mullenax, S. Humphrey, P. Phillips, C. Wilfong, P. Michaels, D. Murphy, and R. Rosier.
Courtesy of Parsons Volunteer Fire Department.

Tucker County Bank
Building, First and
Walnut streets,
Parsons.
Courtesy of Chris Kidwell.

Tucker County Bank.
Courtesy of Chris Kidwell.

The Tucker County Bank,
Third and Walnut streets,
Parsons, organized 1900
postcard.
Courtesy of Chris Kidwell.

Lohr-Barb Funeral Home. *Front row, seated*: Anita and Jeffrey Barb. *Back row, left to right:* Adam Barb, Patrick Thomas, Chris McVean, Hugh DeMotto, Omer Cross, and Nick Barb.

Nick and Adam Barb, 1990, in 1960 S&S Cadillac Funeral Coach.

Interior of Lohr-Barb Funeral Home, Parsons.

Lohr-Barb Funeral Home being built, Main Street, Parsons.

Courtesy of Jeffrey and Anita Barb.

Interior of Lohr-Barb Funeral Home, Parsons.

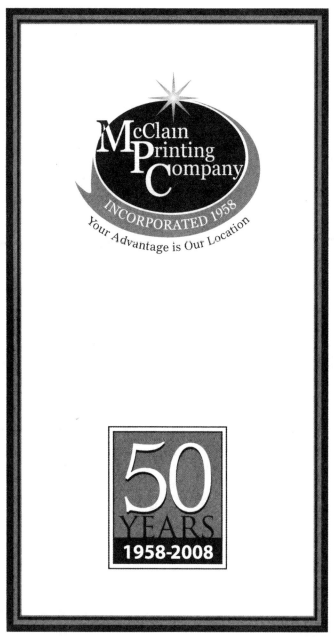

McClain Printing Company
Parsons, WV
Courtesy of McClain Printing Company

Ken McClain circa 1946. Owner and founder of McClain Printing Company.

Ken, Faith, Eddie, Mariwyn and Rachel McClain, 1939, in Morgantown.

C. Faith Reynolds McClain placing letters in the Linotype machine.
Courtesy of Mariwyn McClain Smith.

C. Faith Reynolds McClain 1916-1990.
Courtesy of Mariwyn McClain Smith

Staff and management of McClain Printing Company, circa 2006. *Front row left to right*: Roy Lipscomb, Paul Nestor, Jim Hebb, Steve Lambruno, Bruce Auvil, Mike Griffith, Jack Plum, Charles Marks and Kevin White. *Back row left to right*: Ken Smith, owner and CEO, Robert Leard, Elma Slaubaugh, Melinda Pennington, Shelly McKinnie, Debbie Stemple and Daniel "Chopper" Evans.

Russell Kenneth McClain. (1908-1977).
Courtesy of Mariwyn McClain Smith.

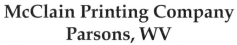

McClain Printing Company
Parsons, WV
Courtesy of McClain Printing Company.

Company Christmas party, 2000, *Front row left to right*: Kayla and Barbie Card, Alisha Nestor, Samantha Adkins, Sarah and Eric Griffith, Billy Plum, Quinn and Elijah Broaddus, Elizabeth and Sarah Smith, Jolena Slaubaugh holding Natalie Holloway, Ethan Slaubaugh, Josh Evans, Cory White, John Taylor Painter, Amber Evans, R.J. Card. *Second row*: Adam and Kelly Young, Deanna Minear, Jack and Susan Plum *holding* Aliyah Plum, Mary Griffith, George Smith, Mariwyn McClain Smith, Barbara Broaddus, Ruth Ann Smith and Ken Smith, Shelly McKinnie, Elma Slaubaugh, Cindy Helmick, Becky and Amber Taylor, and Susan Morrall. *Third row*: Ashley Young, Randy Young, Michael and Melinda Carr, Charles and Carol Hebb, Becky and Kasey Polomski, Mike Griffith, Gail Jones, Vickie Nestor, Andria Auvil, Lori Parsons, Barbie Evans *holding* Natalie Evans, Amanda Simmons, Melinda Lipscomb, Joe Slaubaugh, Todd Oaster, Jeffrey "Buck" Helmick, Angiy Helmick, Eldon Phillips, Rose Phillips. *Back row*: Henry Polomski, Kevin White, David and Chris Nestor, Bruce and Dave Auvil, Daniel "Chopper" Evans, Michael Simmons, Roy Lipscomb and Ray Card.

Ken and George Smith, Barbara Smith Plumley, Faith Smith Robinson and Mariwyn McClain Smith, 1996.

Father and son, former president of MPC George Smith with current president, Ken Smith.
Courtesy of Mariwyn McClain Smith.

**50 Years of
McClain Printing Company
1958-2008
Parsons, WV**
Courtesy of McClain Printing Company.

Staff and management of MPC. *Front row, left to right:* Cory White, Elma Slaubaugh, Shelly McKinnie, George Smith, Mariwyn Smith, Melinda Carr, Mary Griffith, Hillary Morris, and Josh Evans. *Second row:* Kevin White, Ryan DiBacco, John Thompkins, Paul Nestor, Jason Crakes, Robert Leard, Mike Griffith, Roy Lipscomb, Daniel "Chopper" Evans, and Jim Hebb. *Back row:* Larry Martin, Dave Anvil, Ryan Evans, Geoff Martin, Ken Smith, owner and CEO, Asim Islam, Charles Marks, Mike Simmons and Jack Plum.

George, Ken and Mariwyn Smith, celebrating fifty years, 2008.

David Orr, Nancy Parsons, and Joan Hostetler from Mountain Valley Bank helping MPC celebrate.

Public tours of the bindery and pressroom.

Parsons League, "Mulligrubs," postcard.
Courtesy of Chris Kidwell.

Parsons League, "Mulligrubs," 1909 postcard.
Fifth from left in the front row is Joe Parsons.
Courtesy of Chris Kidwell.

Parsons League, Parsons, postcard.
Third from the left on the front row is Chester Barnes.
Courtesy of Chris Kidwell.

Parsons Baseball Team, Parsons, postcard.
Courtesy of Chris Kidwell.

Ball game between Thomas and Parsons, August 8, 1907. Score 24-4 in favor of Parsons, postcard.
Courtesy of Chris Kidwell.

"Making a run, July 3, 1909," postcard.
Courtesy of Chris Kidwell.

Baseball, Parsons, July 3, 1909.
Courtesy of Chris Kidwell.

Grafton vs. Parsons, Parsons.
Courtesy of Chris Kidwell.

Parting of the ways -- wintertime in Parsons, Chestnut and Main streets.
Courtesy of Chris Kidwell.

Holly Meadows, postcard.
Courtesy of Jane H. Barb.

Walnut Street, Parsons.
Courtesy of Jane H. Barb.

Seneca Trail, Parsons,
Shaver's Fork of Cheat, postcard.
Courtesy of Chris Kidwell.

View of Seneca Trail from Backbone Mountain. Altitude 3,000 feet, Parsons, postcard.
Courtesy of Chris Kidwell.

Scene between Hambleton and Parsons.
Courtesy of Chris Kidwell.

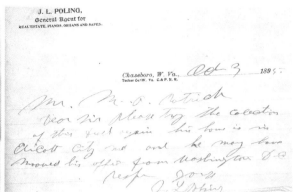

Chaseboro (1895) was located near current St. John's United Methodist Church. It had a post office for three or four years which closed after the bridge was built over Shavers Fork River to Parsons.
Courtesy of Chris Kidwell.

Mill Dam, 1909, Parsons postcard.
Courtesy of Chris Kidwell.

Home of Frank and Lilian Little, Fourth Street, Parsons, August 1950.
Courtesy of Mariwyn McClain Smith.

Electric Light and Power Co.'s Dam, Parsons, postcard.
Courtesy of Chris Kidwell.

Doris Arbogast, Parsons, 1950.
Courtesy of Mariwyn McClain Smith.

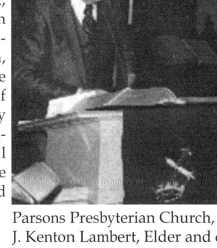

Parsons Presbyterian Church Rev. Troy L. Pritt, Sue Ellen Shrout, Heather Lynn Lee and Barbara Lynne Smith, 1974. The girls are the daughters of David and Mary Ellen Shrout, David and Donell Ridgway Lee and George and Mariwyn McClain Smith.
Courtesy of Mariwyn McClain Smith.

Faith Anne Smith, Christmas Eve, 1976, Parsons Presbyterian Church.
Courtesy of Mariwyn McClain Smith.

Parsons Presbyterian Church, J. Kenton Lambert, Elder and choir director.
Courtesy of Mariwyn McClain Smith.

Katheryn Kite Mauzy and Pauline Rightmire Harris, Parsons Presbyterian Church.
Courtesy of Mariwyn McClain Smith.

Presbyterian Church, Parsons, 1982.
Courtesy of Mariwyn McClain Smith.

Easter 1986, Parsons Prebyterian Church. *Left to right:* Chris, Andy and Michael Manos, Jeff Jones, Brandon Corcoran and Paul Ours.
Courtesy of Mariwyn McClain Smith.

Presbyterian Church, Walnut Street, Parsons, postcard 1910.
Courtesy of Chris Kidwell.

A Message From Our Pastor

The St. John Church of Parsons, West Virginia is a part of the great body of Jesus Christ, reaching out to the people of our community and around the world, serving in Christian love and fellowship. Even as Jesus said, "Inasmuch as ye did it unto one of the least of these my brethren, ye did it unto me." Our Church exists to serve and to be a servant of Jesus. Our church is a people with a vision of the future.

Rev. Paul Fortney

Reverend Paul Fortney, St. Johns United Methodist Church, Parsons.
Courtesy of Chris Kidwell.

Parsons First Methodist Vacation Bible School -- teachers. Katorah Goff and Katherine Poling; minister Rev. Meade Gutshall, July 9-20, 1956.
Courtesy of Chris Kidwell.

Carrie Nation, of the Women's Temperence Movement, visited Parsons in 1908.
Courtesy of Chris Kidwell.

Methodist Protestant Church, Rev. Carl Johnson, pastor, Parsons, postcard. Later St. Johns United Methodist Church.
Courtesy of Chris Kidwell.

Baptist Church, Water Street, Parsons, 1907, postcard.
Courtesy of Chris Kidwell.

M. E. CHURCH SOUTH, PARSONS, W. VA.

Methodist Episcopal Church, South, Parsons
(now St. Paul's United Methodist Church).
Courtesy of Chris Kidwell.

August 1928, Riverview Methodist Church,
Porterwood -- Moran family and others
including *front row fifth from the left*: Jay
Moran; *back row second man from the left*: Russ
Carr; and *man on the farthest right*: Edward
J. Moran.
Courtesy of Chris Kidwell.

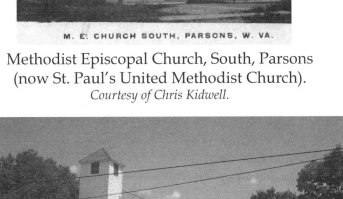

The first St. John's
Church called "Meth-
odist Protestant
Church" circa 1890.
Original photo by J.P.
Maxwell, Parsons.
Courtesy of Chris Kidwell.

St. Paul's United
Methodist Church, 2011.
*Courtesy of
Bill and Linda Evick.*

St. John's Church, Par-
sons. Taking voice les-
sons, *left to right:* Ann
Smithson, Julie Frazee,
Chris Kidwell, Jane Pol-
ing and Jim Poling. Caro-
lyn June Lambert Wilt,
teacher/pianist. Dorothy
O'Neal is pictured. She
was a missionary of the
Methodist Church.
Courtesy of Chris Kidwell.

73rd Annual Session, West Virginia Conference, M.P. Church. WV Photo Company, Thomas/Parsons, September 14-19-1927.
Courtesy of Chris Kidwell.

St. John's United Methodist Bible School, Parsons, WV, circa 1968. *Front row, left to right:* Brian Wilfong, Willetta Swartz, Karen Hockman; *row 2:* Virginia Gray, Dana Hockman, Jill Long, Donna Mullennex, Cathy Martin, Wade Sherman, Eddie Swartz, Scott Hockman, and Mary Alice Phillips; *row 3:* Freda Dumire, Deloris McDonald (standing above Freda), Andrea Felton, Craig Knotts, Mike DeVilder, Jeanette Wamsley, Teresa McDonald, Susie Delaney, Mark Felton, and Annie Good; *row 4:* Grace Wamsley, Mary Alice Hare, Curt Wilfong, Jim McDonald, Chris Kidwell, Randy Strawderman, Eddie Stevens, Dave Stevens, Warren Knotts, Janet Long and Iola Knotts ; *row 5:* _____, Becky Bland, Pam Collins, Pam Long, Charlie Martin, Danny Harman, Rex Lambert and Nola Devilder; *row 6:* Kay Lynn White, Karen Haller, Jack Hockman and John Felton; *row 7:* Eileen Vanscoy Stevens, Diane Wilfong, _____, Dottie Ends, Julie Hockman, Debbie Good, Sandy Hockman, and Joyce Plumley; *row 8:* Annalue Shaffer, Kathy Mullennex, Diane Strawderman, Donna Good, John Doughtery, Clifford Martin, Neal Kidwell, and _____; *back row:* _____, Karolyn Rosier Jones, _____, Frances Harman, and Rev. A.L. Harman.
Courtesy of Chris Kidwell.

Greenlief Funeral Home,
December 27, 1949, Walnut Street,
Parsons.
Courtesy of Mariwyn McClain Smith.

Greenlief-Combs Funeral Home, Parsons.

Independent Order of Odd Fellows (upstairs)
Building, 1949, Parsons. This building was the
United States Post Office in Parsons (downstairs)
in the 1950 and 1960s.

Commencement Exercises

PARSONS HIGH SCHOOL

Parsons High School Auditorium
Wednesday, May 23, 1956
8:00 P. M.

Commencement -- Class of 1956.
Courtesy of Chris Kidwell.

Parsons High School Basketball Team
1953-1954.
Courtesy of Ray and Lucille Adams.

Parsons High School Track Team, 1922.
Front row, left to right: _____,
Clyde Waggy, Virgil Bailey, _____
__, J. Vachon; *middle row, sixth and seventh
from the left:* Ralph Wimer, Jr. and Earl
Corcoran; *back row:* Charles Roberts, ___
_____, _____, Claud Bailey.
Courtesy of Chris Kidwell.

Parsons Graded Public School, 1936-1937.
Miss Ruby Greider, teacher.
Courtesy of Jim and Bob Auvil.

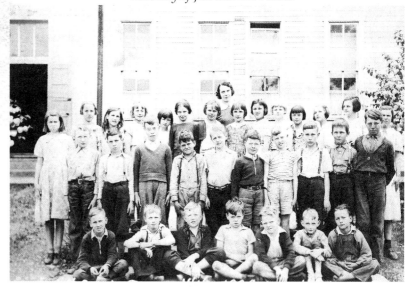

Fourth grade, Parsons, 1939.
Miss Kain Minear, teacher.
Courtesy of Jim and Bob Auvil.

Sixth Grade Basketball Team, Parsons Graded School, Parsons, 1972. *Back row left to right*: Robert Riddle, teacher and coach; Pat Gribble, Jim Poling, Chris Kidwell, Eric Elza and Jimmy Shupp; *middle row*: Malcomb Roy, Bill Stevens, Robert Lantz, Bob Tennant, Fred White, Bob Isner, Jim McDonald, Rick Corcoran, Rocky Shahan and Charlie Sturm, manager; *front row*: Mark Felton, Greg Hott, Curtis Hovatter, John Mahoney, Steve Booth, David Webb, Mark Holler, Hancel Thompson and Paul Pritt.
Courtesy of Chris Kidwell.

Parsons High School Class of 1978 Reunion. *Row 1, left to right:* Sarah Brock Hill, Lois Reinhart, Lois Lipscomb, Debbie Wilson Gehman, Jeanie Knicley Davis, Kennie Felton, Sharon Carr Moats, Chris Kidwell, Becky Nestor Dean, Jesse Dean, Judy Roberts, Judy Pitzer Miller, Joyce Munney Sink. *Row 2:* Ivan Reinhart, Hollis Lipscomb, Dennis Gehman, John Davis, Mark Felton, William Moats, Carolyn Rosier Pifer, Robin Eye, Agnes White Arnold, Clyde Arnold, Bob Roberts, Tom Miller, Robert Sink. *Row 3:* John Mahoney, Kathy Glessner, Diane Mick Elters, Lisa Mauzy Stevens, Bill Stevens, Greg Hott, Allison Hott, Kevin Pifer, Rex Eye, Rick Corcoran, Darlene Pine Green, Tom Lambert, Greg Evans. *Row 4:* Steve Eye, Ronnie Shaffer, Bob Lantz, Sharon Lantz, Robert Knotts, Jeanie Knotts, Dan Dilly, Curtis Wilfong, Kim Michael Wilfong, Dana Hockman Kessler and Hershel Kessler.
Courtesy of Chris Kidwell.

Parsons High School -- Mr. Starkey, coach; Virgil Bailey, sophomore; Claude Bailey, Jr., Leonard
Vachon, Sr., Carl Corbon, Jr., Leo Corrick, Jr., Ralph Wimer, Jr., and McKinley "Pap" Swearingen, Sr.
Courtesy of Chris Kidwell.

Parsons High School, Parsons, postcard.
Courtesy of Chris Kidwell.

Parsons High School, *left to right:*
Lucille D. Kight and Bertie B. Rennix.
Courtesy of Chris Kidwell.

Parsons High School, *back row*: Ralph Wimer, coach; Carl Stemple, Don Griffith, Jack Rowan, George Bowley, and Tracy Nestor. *Front row*: Gerald Repair, Earl Parsons and Herbert Hebb.
Courtesy of Chris Kidwell.

Parsons High School Track Team -- April 20, 1947. *Back row*: Homer Brooks, Jack Gilmore, Billy Piggott, Ross Stemple, Raymond Wilson, Gus Nestor, Donald Good, Pete Ketterman, Donny Poling, Billy Patch, Billy Wingfield, Dick Macy and Bud Helin. *Front row*: Donny Roberts, Kenneth Keller, Rola Cook, Bob Pritt, Bernie Phillips, Jack Rhodes and Truman Phillips.
Courtesy of Chris Kidwell.

Mt. Zion School, 1930s.
Jay Moran, teacher.
Courtesy of Chris Kidwell.

1930s -- Parsons High
School lunch tag Side
#1.

Side #2

Courtesy of Chris Kidwell.

Charles W. Rosenau
Frederick Burton Price
Carole June Orr
Janet Louise Copeland
Elda Mae McDaniel
Franklin Junior Carr
Sylvia Lea Knotts
Juanita Ruth Wilfong
Willetti Wythe Lambert
Charles Edward Sturms
Frank Allan Mullennex
Clark Auvil
Dorothy Mae Barb
Albert Fred Beery
Mary Alice Bell
Donald Eugene Black
William Theodore Bolinger
Donna Jean Carr
Frances Karen Carr
Carrie Louise Dumire
John Alford Evans
Jacqueline Margaret Evick
Paul P. Fansler
Frank Gilbert Ferguson
James Lester Flanagan
Joyce Ann Flynn
Harold Thomas Gray
Harper G. Hamby
Martha Hedrick Sponaugle
Richard B. Hill
Mary Jane Hinkle
William Lee Holler
Morris Ray Jones
Phyllis Faye Jones
Walter Jones
Ponald Eugene Kalar
Zylvia Inetta Kalar
Joseph Earl King
William A. Knotts
Robert Lee Lewis
Ruth Mae Long

Charles Junior Loughry
Grace Louise Loughry
James F. Loughry
Nettie Genevie Loughry
Caryl Ann Lydick
Jack William Miller
Margaret Faye Miller
Betty Jane Myers
Rachel O'Deal McClain
Donald G. Nestor
Naomi Hean Nestor
Agnes Oldaker Poling
Marvin Earl Parsons
Dorris Marylin Pennington
Hoy Vincent Pennington
Clifford Allen Phillips
Edward Gerald Phillips
Joan Miller Phillips
Howard Pyles
Joan Jean Rosier
Richard Lee Roy
Val S. Rudd
Alfred Ray Shahan
Judith Ellen Shields
Philip Alan Shrout
Florence Ann Simmons
Paul William Sponaugle
Ida Jane Stemple
Lawrence G. Stevens
Dale C. Nestor
Grace Nina Anne Taylor
Sara Pauline Trigg
Tom Marion Watring
Velda Mae Watring
Keith Wilfong
Richmond Bell Williams
Ruth Williams
Christena Carol Sponaugle
Coy Jacob Wolford
Luther Baskium Woods, Jr.
James Bonner

Harry Sommerville

Parsons High School list of names for Commencement 1956.

SCHOOL DAYS

1947-48

Ruth Mullenax (Mauzy).
1947-1948.
Courtesy of Delain Mullenax.

Lisa Mauzy (Wilfong), Parsons.
Daughter of Paul and Ruth
Mullenax Mauzy.
Courtesy of Delain Mullenax.

Hobson School,
Jay Moran, teacher.
Courtesy of Chris Kidwell.

Sixth grade class in 1973 at Parsons Graded School. *Front row, left to right*: Linda Shirley, Anna Lee Phillips, Jeanny Knicely, Rose Ann Miller, Kim Michael, Teresa Close, Robin Plum, Debra Moore, Sandra Whitt, Amanda Whetzle, Rosey Boyles, Darlene Pine, Lisa Mauzy and Dana Hockman; *second row*: Mrs. King, Mike Bohon, Greg Evans, Ricky Phillips, Pat Gribble, Deloris Cross, Becky Nestor, Janet Phillips, Debra Nestor, Agnes White, Marsha Persutti, Linda Cassidy, Amanda Judy, Joyce Murray, Charlotte Bucklew, Percilla Simmons, Debra White, Darlene Myers, Judy Pitzer, DiAnn Hovatter, Mr. Hansford (Coon Hunter); *third row*: Mr. Riddle, Steve Eye, Denver Roy, Rex Eye, Malcomb Roy, James Poling, Mark Bright, David Webb, Hancel Thompson, Robert Tennet, Steve Booth, John Mahoney, Greg Hott, Charles Sturms, Eric Elza, Mark Felton; *fourth row*: Fred White, Jimmy Shupp, Jerry Phillips, Chris Kidwell, Robinson Long, Paul Pritt, Robert Isner, James McDonald, Ricky Corcoran, Billy Stevens, Robert Knotts, Bob Lantz, David Bolinger, Ricky Dumire, Billy Holler, Rocky Shahan and Curtis Hovatter. *Courtesy of Kim Michael Wilfong.*

Parsons High School, student office help, 1946-1947. *Front row left to right:* Colleen Dudley, Margaret Ann Felton, Erma Bible and Rosalie Marteney; *back row left to right:* Evelyn Hebb, JoAnn White, Jean Sturm, Maurice Freeman, principal. *Courtesy of Evelyn Chaney.*

Parsons High School Spanish Club, 1946-1947. *Front row left to right:* Gloria Pinkerton, Julia Kisner, Mary Alice Frum, teacher, Evelyn Hebb and Eula Bright; *back row:* Burton Cornell, Kenneth Keller and Richard Higgs. *Courtesy of Evelyn Chaney.*

Mr. P.H.S. 1973, Robert James Hebb.
Courtesy of Chris Kidwell.

Parsons High School 1922 basketball players. *Back row*: Virgil Bailey, Darwin Chase and Joe Vachon. *Front row*: Ralph Wimer and "Buss" Claud Bailey.
Courtesy of Chris Kidwell.

School Building, River Street, Parsons, postcard.
Courtesy of Chris Kidwell.

Jim Barr, Parsons High School gymnasium, Parsons, 1957, postcard.
Courtesy of Chris Kidwell.

First grade, Parsons Graded School, 1935; Miss Flanagan, teacher.
Courtesy of Mariwyn McClain Smith.

Fifth grade, Parsons Graded School, 1935; Miss Wise, teacher.
Courtesy of Mariwyn McClain Smith.

Parsons High School -- 1928. *Back row:* Blake Simmons, Leon Kelly, Tracy Nestor, Carl Lipscomb, Ancile Gray, Denzil Kee, Harry Phillips, Dick Evick, Doyle Schoonover, Paul Parsons, George Miller, Ralph Wimer, coach. *Front row:* Fritz Wagner, Wilbur Minear, Junior "Hornet" Stalnaker, Earl Parsons, Jack Rowan, Harper "Doc" Wimer, and Wade Poffenbarger.
Courtesy of Chris Kidwell.

Parsons High School

BASKETBALL SCHEDULE

Dec. 25—Alumni	Home
Dec. 28—Jane Lew	There
Dec. 29—New Martinsville,	Home
Jan. 1—Linsly Institute (Wheeling)	Home
Jan. 4—Tygarts Valley	There
Jan. 7—Petersburg	Home
Jan. 11—Belington	There
Jan. 14—Jane Lew	Home
Jan. 21—Elkins	Home
Jan. 25—Elkins	There
Jan. 28—Thomas	Home
Feb. 4—Tygarts Valley	Home
Feb. 8—Coalton	There
Feb. 11—Belington	Home
Feb. 16—Keyser	Home
Feb. 18—Thomas	There
Feb. 23—Coalton	Home
Feb 25—Franklin	There
Feb. 26—Petersburg	There
Mar. 2—Circleville	Home
Mar. 4—Keyser	There

MYRL KEPNER, Coach.
CECIL SIMMONS, Mgr.

Parsons High School -- 1927. *Back row:* Berkie Senior, Jack Rowan, Junior "Hornet" Stalnaker, Ralph Wimer, coach. *Front row:* Harper "Doc" Wimer, Earl Parsons and Wilbur Minear.
Courtesy of Chris Kidwell.

Teacher, Jay Moran at Halloween.
Courtesy of Chris Kidwell.

Parsons High School, 1920. *Front row, left to right:* Florence Simpson, Ruth Wood, Vanyla Swartz, Violet Summerfield, Fern Brown, Gene Orr and Mary Scott; *middle row*: Lucille Freeman, Harry Mateer, John Moran, Harry Poling, Harry Kelly and Marie Auvil; *back row*: Ernest Vachon, Guy Rolley, and Frank Higgs.
Courtesy of Chris Kidwell.

Patty Goff and Sally Ann English, 1947.
Courtesy of Kim Michael Wilfong.

Left to right: Clyde Lester Bell, Jay Moran, Harley Lee Watson and Denver Lee Rosier -- Harper School first grade.
Courtesy of Chris Kidwell.

Parsons High School Basketball Team, 1918, postcard. *Front row, left to right:* Ernest Vachon, Cecil Phillips and "Pap" McKinley Swearingen. *Back row*: Pat Vachon, Harry Mateer, Harry Colebank, Dale Biddle and Dale Ryan.
Courtesy of Chris Kidwell.

Demolition of Parsons Graded School.
Courtesy of Kim Michael Wilfong.

Parsons High School senior girls' basketball team, 1946-1947. *Left to right:* Hazel Hull, teacher-sponsor, Joan Funkhouser, Erma Bible, Margaret Ann Felton, Julia Kisner, Rosalie Marteney, Evelyn Hebb, Gloria Pinkerton, and Mary Alice Frum, teacher-coach. *Courtesy of Evelyn Chaney.*

Parsons High School, National Honor Society initiation of new members, 1946-1947. *Left to right*: Evelyn Hebb, Nellie Painter, Julia Kisner, Joanna Felton, JoAnn White, Jean Sturm, Willis Williams and William Watring.
Courtesy of Evelyn Chaney.

Mary Hebb, Parsons High School senior photo, 1940. Mary Emily Hebb, daughter of Thomas and Stella Lipscomb Hebb, was born on the family farm on Hile Run. When she finished eighth grade at the Hickory Grove school she couldn't go on to high school because there was no adequate transportation. When the school bus route from Leadmine to the high school in Parsons was established in 1936, Mary walked the mile and a half trail and dirt road to meet the school bus. This meant leaving before full daylight and getting home in the evening's dusk. The family moved into Leadmine in October 1936. Mary was graduated with the senior class from Parsons High School in May 1940. She lived her adult life in St. George.
Courtesy of Evelyn Chaney.

WAYNE K. PRITT
ATTORNEY AND COUNSELOR AT LAW
PARSONS, W. VA.

April 1, 1922.

Mr. H. S. Shaffer,
Grey, Pa.

Dear Sir:

The 125 acre farm of Thomas P. Propst, upon which you hold a deed of trust for about $300 00, as I am informed, is advertised to be sold on May 1, 1922. This sale is to be made under a prior deed of trust executed to J. P. Scott, Trustee, for a note owing to W. J. Digman.

There seem to be three deeds of trust, which are prior to yours; the total indebtedness aggregating approximately $1000 00, including the probable cost of sale. It would seem that it would be necessary for you to interest yourself in this sale to protect your interests, and with that in view to see that the property brings an amount equal to the indebtedness against it.

Mr. Harvey Auvil and myself are sureties on a renewal note of $80 00 for Mr. Propst, which is secured by a deed of trust prior to yours, and this is what brought the matter to our attention. Therefore, it occurred to us that it might be well to write you on the subject, although you may have seen the advertisement in the Democrat.

This property has been for sometime listed with Mr. Young and myself for sale at the price of $1600 00, and $1000 00 would seem to be a sacrifice price.

Very truly yours,

WKP:IVA

Letter from Attorney, Wayne K. Pritt, 1922.
Courtesy of Chris Kidwell.

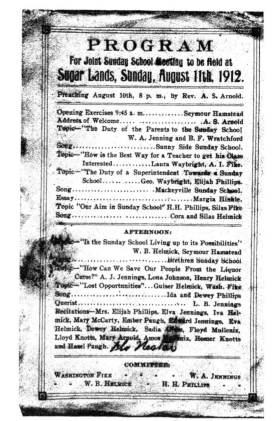

Program at Sugarlands
Sunday School Class, 1912.
Courtesy of Chris Kidwell.

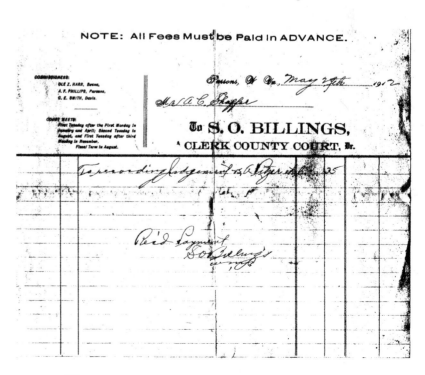

S.O. Billings Clerk County Court
Dr. Court fees, 1912.
Courtesy of Chris Kidwell.

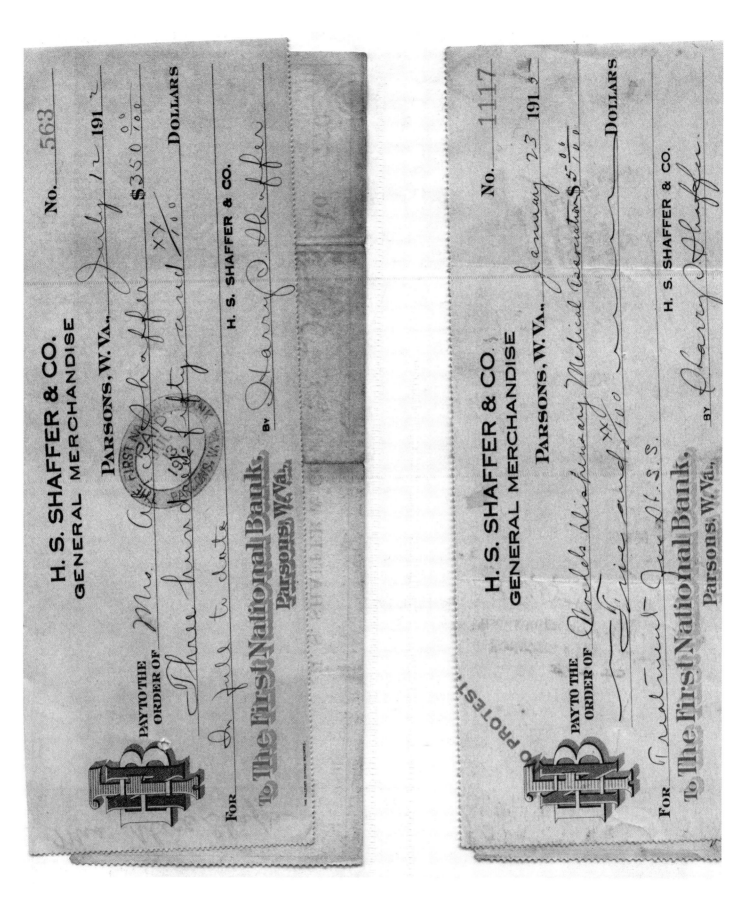

H.S. Shaffer & Co. General Merchandise -- checks 1912 and 1915.
Courtesy of Chris Kidwell.

TUCKER COUNTY FAIR ASSOCIATION

L. W. PARSONS, PRESIDENT
F. G. T. FERGUSON, VICE PRESIDENT
H. S. SHAFFER, SECRETARY
RILEY HARPER, TREASURER.

PARSONS, W. VA.......................191

1912
aug 21 — D Horse +B. 2da   2.50
Nov. 11 — . . b   2.?0

1913
March 21   D Horse   3.00
May 4   " Horse + Buggy   4.00
Nov. 24   " "   2.50

1911
July 18   D Horse   ⎱ 1.50
                           ⎰   75
Dec 22   " Horse   4.00
Jan 31   By Check   400

Tucker County Fair Association,
1917.
Courtesy of Chris Kidwell.

Program for Farmers' Institute,
1912.
Courtesy of Chris Kidwell.

FIRST DAY, 10:00 A. M.

Devotional Exercises.

Music by the Choir.

Maintaining the Soil Fertility ....E. Diefenbach

Lime ....J. F. Gordon

Question Box.

NOON RECESS.

AFTERNOON SESSION, 1:30 P. M.

Possibilities of an Acre of Land ....E. Diefenbach

Soil Improvement ....J. F. Gordon

How to Teach Agriculture in the Public Schools ....R. E. King

Music

SECOND DAY, 10:00 A. M.

Devotional Exercises.

Big Money From Little Things ....E. Diefenbach

Drainage ....J. F. Gordon

Query Box.

Discussion.

NOON RECESS.

AFTERNOON SESSION.

Music.

Corn Culture ....E. Diefenbach

Alfalfa ....J. F. Gordon

Music by the Choir.

Election of Officers.

ADJOURNMENT.

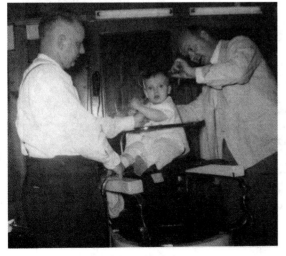

Wade Kidwell, Neal Kidwell (first haircut) and
Worley Simmons, barber, Second Street, Parsons.
Courtesy of Chris Kidwell.

PROGRAM

FOR

FARMERS' INSTITUTE

TO BE HELD AT

HOLLY MEADOW CHURCH

TUCKER COUNTY, W. VA.

SEPTEMBER 19-20, 1912

UNDER THE AUSPICES OF THE

STATE BOARD OF AGRICULTURE

INSTRUCTORS.—J. F. GORDON, Jamestown, Ohio.
E. DIEFENBACH, Huntington, W. Va.

OFFICERS.—J. A. H. SWISHER, *President*.
C. W. LONG, *Secretary*.

Program for Farmers' Institute, 1912.
Courtesy of Chris Kidwell.

Nora Flanagan, Patricia Judy, Carol Kidwell, Jeannie Hehle Ledden and Bert Price at 113 Center Street, Quality Hill, home of J.W. Kidwell.
Courtesy of Chris Kidwell.

Nick Barb and Jim Michael.
Courtesy of Jim and Bob Auvil.

Alfred Shahan, Ernie Price and Bittie Hanlan building Ernie's house, 1977.
Courtesy of Chris Kidwell.

Haskell Schilansky, grocery store owner in Parsons, 1980.
Courtesy of Chris Kidwell.

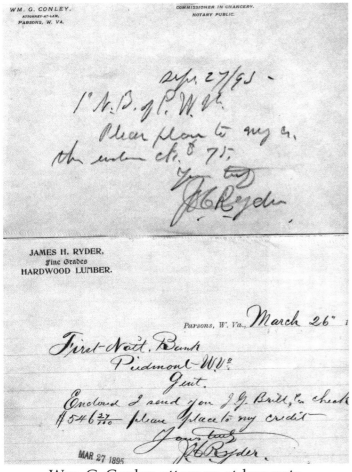

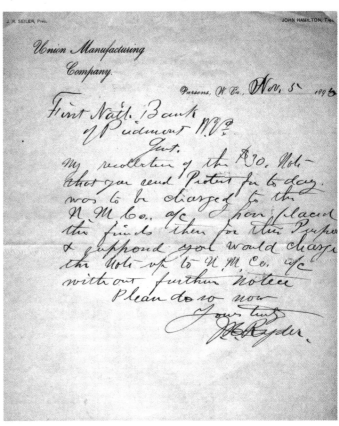

Union Manufacturing Note, 1895.
Courtesy of Chris Kidwell.

Wm. G. Conley, attorney-at-law note
and James H. Ryder note, 1895.
Courtesy of Chris Kidwell.

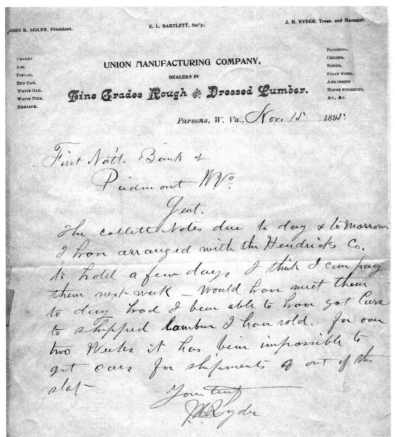

Isom Judy and his pet "coon," Arnold,
Fork Mountain.
Courtesy of Chris Kidwell.

Union Manufacturing Note, 1895.
Courtesy of Chris Kidwell.

Photo at Pheasant Run, on the West Virginia C&P Railroad, in Tucker County, five miles southeast of Parsons, the county seat, and nearest bank location, and two miles from Porterwood, its shipping point. Mail, daily. E.J. Moran, postmaster. Allendar, T.A., carpenter, Atwell & Lockhard, saw mill, Canfield, L.G. carpenter, Channel, Sylvester, miller, Deer, Mary, teacher, Irons, A.J., livestock, Moran, E.J., general store, Parsons, C.R., teacher and Parsons, T.B., livestock.
Courtesy of Chris Kidwell.

"Lucy and Ethel" -- Dess Kidwell and Bert Price, January 31, 1958.
Courtesy of Chris Kidwell.

Betty Bright and _____
Courtesy of Jim and Bob Auvil.

Back row, far right: Margaret and Edward J. Moran -- Moran Family.
Courtesy of Chris Kidwell.

Moran home, Pheasant Run.
Left to right: Margaret, Jay and Edward J. Moran.
Courtesy of Chris Kidwell.

Unknown World War II soldier,
Parsons.
Courtesy of Chris Kidwell.

Fawley Building Fire,
Main Street, Parsons,
May 21, 1932.
Courtesy of Chris Kidwell.

Note the A& P
Store Sign.

Fire of Fawley Building, 317 First Street, Parsons, May 21, 1932.

Cleta M. Long, 1936-2000, author of five books.

Becky Smith (Bromell) Parsons High School, Class of 1955.
Courtesy of Dixie Goff Gutmann.

W.H. Dasher and S.D. Williams had a dairy at Moore, WV, late 1800s and early 1900s. Only two of these bottles are known to be in existence.
Courtesy of Chris Kidwell.

E.J. Getz, Pheasant Run, Jay Moran's brother-in-law, World War II.
Courtesy of Chris Kidwell.

Nelson's Tree Service, out of Dayton, OH, 1950. *Left to right*: Bill Judy, Junior Wyford and Dale Kelly. Bob Jones was foreman. They cut trees in Parsons, Thomas, Davis, Elkins, Belington and Marlinton.
Courtesy of Chris Kidwell.

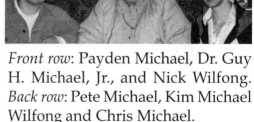

Front row: Payden Michael, Dr. Guy H. Michael, Jr., and Nick Wilfong. *Back row*: Pete Michael, Kim Michael Wilfong and Chris Michael.
Courtesy of Kim Michael Wilfong.

Mrs. Josie Parsons (third grade), Mrs. Morrison (first grade), Parsons Graded School.
Courtesy of Chris Kidwell.

Newly-built Kidwell's Machine Shop, Parsons, July 1984. Josh Kidwell. (Edith Arbogast's home in background.)
Courtesy of Chris Kidwell.

Paul Mauzy, Jr., 1956-1957. Son of Paul and Ruth Mullenax Mauzy.
Courtesy of Delain Mullenax.

Jackie Irons, Agnes White and Cindy Wilson behind old grade school during recess.
Courtesy of Chris Kidwell.

Delbert Ball, World War II, Parsons.
Courtesy of Chris Kidwell.

1950 neighbors on Quality Hill. *Left to right*: Wade Kidwell, Worley Simmons, Isabel Simmons, Marg Gray, Pat Gray and Buck Gray.
Courtesy of Chris Kidwell.

120

Tucker Democrat, First Street, Parsons. Purchased by Ken McClain
in early 1950s and became part of *The Parsons Advocate.*
Courtesy of Chris Kidwell.

Minear's Livery in Parsons -- J.W. Minear, Agent, Anchor &
Lion Buggies, Weber Wagons. *Left to right:* John W. Minear
(1872-1945), Fire Chief Phil Kee, M. Wade Phillips, Jim Hul-
ings, A.P. Cunningham, Ova Cross, Amer E. Lake, Robert W.
Parsons and Troy Lake.
Courtesy of Jane H. Barb.

David "Boots" Humphrey with his car
broken down along the Dry Fork River,
circa 1972.
Courtesy of Chris Kidwell.

Odd Fellows, Parsons. *Back, left to right:* Ray Jenkins, Charlie Miller, Elliott "Fats" Ryan, Leo Goss, Daily Martin, Stark Johnson, Clarence Loughry, Lloyd Phillips, _____, Fred Long and Isom Judy. *Front row:* Richard VanMeter, Charlie Buchanan, Carl M. Hedrick (sheriff), John Campbell, _____, John Wilson, Roy Phillips, Gaston Poling, Dallas Propst and Richard Pennington.
Courtesy of Chris Kidwell.

Left to right: Katorah Goff, Eve Goff Channel, Lena Goff Jones, Grace Goff Gilmore and Elsie Goff Davis.
Courtesy of Kim Michael Wilfong.

Left to right: Sheila Parsons, Pete and Kim Michael, Joe DiBacco, Kim Parsons and stray cat.
Courtesy of Kim Michael Wilfong.

Dr. Guy H. Michael, Sr.
Courtesy of Kim Michael Wilfong.

Mrs. James (Patricia Goff) Michael.
Courtesy of Kim Michael Wilfong.

122

Marvin and Earl Knotts, Knotts' Reunion, 1984.
Courtesy of Delain Mullenax.

Delton Knotts, Knotts' Reunion, August 29, 1982.
Courtesy of Delain Mullenax.

Cub Scouts at Grace and Bob Minear's home. *Front, left to right:* ____ George, Dick Kidwell, Lanny West, Dave Shrout, Bill Minear, Tuck Sherman; *back row:* Gary Corcoran, Craig Simmons, Gary Simmons, Ross Simmons, Mr. and Mrs. Minear, 1950.
Courtesy of Chris Kidwell.

Claude and Arthur "Arth" Knotts, Knotts' Reunion, August 26, 1984.
Courtesy of Delain Mullenax.

Frank, Jean (Varner), Debbie and Frank, Jr. Mullenax, 1962.
Courtesy of Delain Mullenax.

Kidwell Auto Parts employees, Christmas 1976. *Back row, left to right:* Dess Kidwell, vice president, Dick K. Kidwell, manager, Craig Wilfong, Neal Kidwell and Lawrence Ends; *front row:* John Lambert, Sharon Kidwell, Doris Kisamore, and Wade Kidwell, president.
Courtesy of Chris Kidwell.

John Wade Kidwell, owner, Kidwell Auto Parts, 413 First Street, Parsons, 1954. His first store opened April 4, 1946, beside C.W. Harvey Building.
Courtesy of Chris Kidwell.

Rachel McClain Wright 1953-1954 school photo.
Courtesy of Mariwyn McClain Smith.

Knotts' Reunion, 1993, Sugarlands. *Left to right:* Sylvia, Kenny, Perry, Alva, Irene, Harry and Junior Knotts.
Courtesy of Delain Mullenax.

Leecie and Lillie Helmick Mullenax.
Courtesy of Delain Mullenax.

Nick Wilfong of Parsons -- professionally known by his acting stage name of Nick Bolton.
Courtesy of Kim Michael Wilfong.

Debbie Knotts, Ruth Mauzy and Delain Mullenax, Knotts' Reunion in Sugarlands, August 26, 1984.
Courtesy of Delain Mullenax.

Frank and Delton Mullenax, December 1986.
Courtesy of Delain Mullenax.

Kim Michael (Wilfong) and Lisa Mauzy (Wilfong).
Courtesy of Kim Michael Wilfong.

Tucker County Fair, Parsons, Coronation of Queen Daphne. *Pictured are:* UK Guy H.
Michael, Sr., Charles Wagner, UK Dave Gatrell, Effie Jane Pennington, Mary Alice
Miller, Bruce Vance, Patty Goff, Charles Kines, Barbara Colabrese, Sonny Ours, Nick
Barb, UK Josephine Hehle, Macel Carr, Henry Thompson, UK Ernie Moon, UK Earl
Corcoran, and ring bearer Frank Ours. Parsons firemen served as escorts.
Courtesy of Jane H. Barb.

Tucker County Fair parade,
honoring Queen Daphne and her court, 1954.
Courtesy of Mariwyn McClain Smith.

Annabelle Parsons, 1930s water fountain
built by Works Progress Administration,
at Parsons courthouse.
Courtesy of Chris Kidwell.

The first automobile in Tucker County was owned by Mr. and Mrs. Richard Shaffer of Baltimore, MD, formerly of St. George, and driven by them from Baltimore to St. George, in 1902, taking eight days to complete the trip.

Tucker County Fair Program -- 1960.

Courtesy of Chris Kidwell.

Father of the Fair

JOHN T. REGER

Founder of the Tucker County Fair, he was born in Philippi, W. Va., December 24, 1858, and died in Belington, W. Va., January 6, 1937, age 78 years. He was a newspaper editor and publisher, band leader, accomplished musician, and very active in civic affairs. Edited and published The Plaindealer in Philippi for a number of years and was editor and publisher of The Tucker Democrat in Parsons from July 1907 to July 1917. Organized the Tucker County Fair in 1914 and was its first Secretary.

Queen of Hearts

MRS. DOVE CORRICK
Chairman of the Prize Committee for the past 24 years (since 1936).

"Has given away a fortune in prizes"

Queen of Queens

MRS. VIRGINIA SCHRECONGOST
Chairman of the Queen Committee and President of the Parsons Fire Department Auxiliary.

"Prepares the Queens for their Reigns"

126

Welcome to the Tucker County Fair

The Tucker County Fair, fun on the Midway, and coronation of the Queen are provided jointly by the Tucker County Fair Association and the Parsons Volunteer Fire Department.

Eighty per cent of the net proceeds of this gala affair will go to the fire department to provide funds for the purchase of fire fighting equipment necessary for the protection of our community. Your patronage is earnestly solicited and you are assured that the money you spend with us will be used for a worthy cause, that of providing you with a modern and efficient volunteer fire department.

We thank all our advertisers who made this program possible and request the public to patronize them at every opportunity.

FAIR OFFICIALS

President	Carl R. Barr
Vice President	Fontz Jones
Secretary Pro-tempore	Homer Floyd Fansler
Treasurer	Gordon Shrader

FIRE DEPARTMENT OFFICIALS

President	William Harlow
Vice President	Fontz Jones
Secretary	Larry Mayfield
Treasurer	John Filler
Fire Chief	Darl Stalnaker
First Assistant Fire Chief	James Propst
Second Assistant Fire Chief	Clarence Bohon
Captain	Paul Fansler
First Lieutenant	Willard Caldwell
Second Lieutenant	(vacant)
Sergeant-at-Arms	(vacant)
Chaplain	Alba Mitchell

Illustration of Long's Department Store, First Street, Parsons. Oldest building still in existence in Tucker County. Now (2011) owned and operated by Ben F. Long; established by his grandfather, B. Frank Long.
Courtesy of Ben Long.

Tucker County Fair Program -- 1960.
Courtesy of Chris Kidwell.

QUEEN DAPHNE XX

Miss Patricia Dime
Daughter of Mr. and Mrs. Jean R. Golightly of Davis

MAIDS-OF-HONOR

Miss Juanita Armentrout
Daughter of Mr. and Mrs.
Hencie Armentrout of Davis

Miss Barbara Quattro
Daughter of Mr. and Mrs.
Rocco Quattro of Davis

127

The Census

BY HOMER FLOYD FANSLER

In March 1959, this writer published the following predictions in his Decennial Census booklet: "The United States is expected to gain 25 million people since the last census of 1950. West Virginia is not expected to lose population but is expected to be reapportioned to the extent that it will reduce her membership in the House of Representatives from six to five and thereby do away with one West Virginia Congressman. Tucker County is expected to lose 1,600 persons and wind up the next census with a population of 9,000. These figures are a 'Fearless Forecast by Fansler,' based on a careful study of business trends, migration of labor, and vital statistics."

The Census of 1960 has been taken and it appears that this writer was neither fearless nor careful in his studies of trends, migration and statistics. His prediction concerning the United States is almost a bull's-eye but his predictions for West Virginia and Tucker County are something from the other end of the bull. The United States gained 26½ million, West Virginia lost 157,616, and Tucker County lost 2,849. Parsons lost 236; this writer made no prediction on Parsons, had he done so he would have lost on that, too, as he thought Parsons would gain instead of lose. There's not a vacant house in Parsons.

The population of Tucker County dropped to 7,751 and at the Primary Election, last May, there were 5,845 registered voters in Tucker County, which leaves only 1,906 minors. The enrollment in the County's schools, last year, was 1,900, and this doesn't include children under six years of age. How then do we reconcile these figures? Are the dead being carried on the rolls of registered voters? No, the answer lies in the fact that many are registered to vote in Tucker County who do not reside in Tucker County. If this trend continues, and apparently it will, Tucker County will soon have more registered voters than it has population.

Census figures from 1900 to 1960, for the incorporated towns of Tucker County, the County, and the State, are as follows:

	1900	1910	1920	1930	1940	1950	1960
West Va.	958,800	1,221,119	1,463,701	1,729,205	1,901,974	2,005,552	1,847,936
Tucker Co.	13,433	18,675	16,791	13,374	13,173	10,600	7,751
Davis	2,208	3,200	2,491	1,656	1,454	1,271	894
Hambleton	306	912	488	388	394	283	275
Hendricks	502	750	622	484	539	492	407
Parsons	839	1,780	2,001	2,012	2,146	2,009	1,773
Thomas	1,424	2,398	2,099	1,660	1,448	1,146	834

Tucker County Fair Program -- 1960.
Courtesy of Chris Kidwell.

Isom Judy and David Lee Kidwell, circa 1950s, during Tucker County Fair. David won first place in the parade.
Courtesy of Chris Kidwell.

Brother and sister, Virginia and Paul Mauzy at Tucker Country Inn, 1990.
Courtesy of Delain Mullenax.

Crowd at Camp Kidd during Republican Arch Moore rally.
Courtesy of Kim Michael Wilfong.

Tucker County Fair Program -- 1960.
Courtesy of Chris Kidwell.

The Fair
BY HOMER FLOYD FANSLER

America's first Fair was held October 1, 1810, in Pittsfield, Mass. It was sponsored by 26 civic leaders, particularly interested in the livestock side of farming, and they urged the farmers "to exhibit on the Square, in the village of Pittsfield, their cattle, sheep and swine of different breeds and grades." From this first farm animal show have sprung the 2,000 or more agricultural Fairs which take place every year in the United States. Every State in the Union, except Nevada and Vermont, have annual State Fairs.

The Tucker County Fair Association was organized in 1914, by John T. Reger of Parsons and William H. Ryan of Hendricks. A membership fee of $1.00 per year was assessed, which entitled the member to a badge and a card certifying membership, free entry to the Fair grounds and exhibits, and a legitimate voice by vote in the business affairs of the organization. The membership fee has long since been dropped and the business affairs are so conducted that just anybody can attend the meetings and vote on procedures and activities, thereby enabling cliques, controls and fixes to be established at will. The Association was incorporated December 6, 1927, with fifteen charter members, ten of which are now deceased. All Fair accounts are audited annually by the State Auditor's Office. A photostat of the Charter appears with this article.

Rodney A. Barb at F.S. Johnsons's Drugstore, Parsons.
Courtesy of Jane H. Barb.

Crowd at Republican Arch Moore rally.
Courtesy of Kim Michael Wilfong.

Children's Egg Toss
at the Hick Festival at Camp Kidd.
Courtesy of Delain Mullenax.

Kenny Currence (*with hat and glasses*), Charlie
Wine and Barry Clutter, *seated on right,* during
the One-Man Saw contest at the Hick Festival
at Camp Kidd. Labor Day weekend, 1990.
Courtesy of Delain Mullenax.

Hick Festival announcer, Foster Mullenax autographing one
of his novels at the Hick Festival where he was the master of
ceremonies for many years, as well as the voice of the State Fair
of West Virginia.
Courtesy of Delain Mullenax.

"Coon" chase on the water at the
Hick Festival, Camp Kidd, 1991.
Courtesy of Delain Mullenax.

Sylvia Mullenax and Velma Knotts at
the Hick Festival, Holly Meadows, 1991.
Courtesy of Delain Mullenax.

Parsons Courthouse. Band members shown, *left to right*, Jules "Dittle" Cross, Elliott "Fats" Ryan and Casey Jones (playing trumpet). Governor Guy Kump in the center on podium.

Courtesy of Chris Kidwell.

In memory of all American Veterans, July 20, 2005. The wall was completely designed and built by volunteers.
Courtesy of Delain Mullenax.

Parade, Parsons,
July 3, 1909.
Courtesy of Chris Kidwell.

Crowd awaiting parade.
Courtesy of Chris Kidwell.

Parade, Parsons,
July 3, 1909, postcard.
Courtesy of Chris Kidwell.

"Still Rockin' After 50 Years" McClain Printing Company, Parsons. Parsons Volunteer Firemen's Spring Fling Parade, May 10, 2008.

Left to right: Shelly McKinnie, Melinda Carr, Ken Smith, Mike Griffith, George and Mariwyn Smith, Ethan Carr and Samantha Long.

Ken Smith.

Photos courtesy of McClain Printing Company.

George and Mariwyn Smith with *left to right:* Ethan and Mary Beth Carr, Makala, Samantha and Abigail Long and, *at far right*, Taylor McKinnie.

West Virginia Central Train wreck, Pulp Mill Bottom, June 26, 1926, Parsons.
Courtesy of Chris Kidwell.

J.K. Mosser Co. tanneries, Parsons, postcard.
Courtesy of Chris Kidwell.

View of United States Forest
Service, Parsons, postcard
-- *Courtesy of Chris Kidwell.*

Largest Nursery East of Mississippi River

GUEST CARD

PARSONS, WEST VIRGINIA

"The Flame Azalea City"

WELCOMES YOU AND HOPES YOU
WILL RETURN OFTEN

THIS CARD ENTITLES YOU TO PARK YOUR
CAR AS LONG AS YOU LIKE WHILE A GUEST
OF OUR CITY. OUR POLICE OFFICERS WILL
EXTEND YOU EVERY COURTESY.

For Additional Information Call The Tucker County
Bank; F. S. Johnston Drug Store; Sheriff's Office or
City Council Hall.

APPROVED BY THE MAYOR
AND CITY COUNCIL

VISIT THE FOLLOWING POINTS
OF INTEREST AROUND PARSONS

1. **U. S. GOVERNMENT NURSERY:**—Largest east of the Mississippi River; Home of C. C. C. Camp Parsons.
2. **CORRICK'S FORD BATTLEFIELD:**—Where the First Officer of the Civil War Was Killed.
3. **ST. GEORGE:**—The First County Seat of Tucker County; Scene of Civil War Conflicts; Indian Mound and Graves Near This Town.
4. **HORSESHOE CAMP:**—U. S. Forest Camp; Swimming, Picnic, Tent and Trailer Camp (Open May 30 to Labor Day) Located on Horseshoe Run and the Earliest Traveled Road in Tucker County.
5. **SENECA TRAIL:**—Famous Indian Trail Which Crosses Backbone Mountain.
6. **BLACKWATER CANYON:**—Equal to any River Gorge in the East.
7. **FAIRFAX STONE:**—Spot Surveyed By Lord Fairfax and George Washington.
8. **BLACKWATER FALLS:**—65-Foot Scenic Wonder of West Vrginia.
9. **CANAAN VALLEY:**—Bowl 13 Miles Long; Seen Best from Canaan Lookout Tower.
10. **PARSONS TANNERY:**—One of Armour Company's Best Plants.
    DORMAN MILLS:—Manufacturers of High Class Woolen Products.

COMPLIMENTS OF
RIVER CITY CLUB
LOCAL MEN'S CIVIC ORGANIZATION
PARSONS, WEST VIRGINIA

Guest card for US Forest Nursery, Parsons, sides one and two.
Courtesy of Chris Kidwell.

YMCA Camp Horseshoe

Courtesy of Chris Kidwell.

Dining Hall, postcard, 1955.

Swimming area, postcard, 1953.

Camp Horseshoe.
Courtesy of Jane H. Barb.

Athletic Field, 1956.

YMCA Camp Horseshoe
Courtesy of Chris Kidwell.

Camp Cook's Quarters, postcard.

"Staff at Y.M.C.A. Camp Horseshoe, Parsons, W.Va."

Western Maryland Railroad at Parsons, circa 1960s. Stopped, getting ready to make a run up Blackwater Canyon, Parsons Depot is in the background.
Courtesy of Chris Kidwell.

Civilian Conservation Corps train stopping in Parsons, circa 1930s.
Courtesy of Chris Kidwell.

Survivors' Lap, 2005, at R.H. Armstrong Memorial Field.

Mary Beth Carr and Taylor McKinnie
walking the track for a cure.

**Tucker County American Cancer Society
Relay For Life
2005**
Courtesy of McClain Printing Company.

McClain Printing
Company tent.
Left to right:
Melinda Carr, Elma
Slaubaugh and
Mariwyn Smith.

The "kitchen crew"-- volunteers for the July 4, 2010, golden wedding anniversary celebration of George and Mariwyn Smith included *left to right*: Betty Snyder Bonner, Terry George Gsell, Jennifer Jones Greenlief, Cathy Bonner Lee, Jean Nester Corcoran Long and Kelly Corcoran Underwood.
Courtesy of Mariwyn McClain Smith.

Parsons Centennial booklet, June 12, 1893-June 12, 1993.
Courtesy of Jane Barb.

Fifty years after graduating from Parsons High School, five 1955 classmates and their spouses went on a cruise to Bermuda. Those attending were *left to right*: George and Mariwyn Smith, of Parsons, Gary and Sonia Hovatter of Baltimore, Okey and Mary Moore of Parsons, Frank and Sharlene Day Carr of Leadmine and Akron, and Marvin "Bud" and Jane Hinebaugh Parsons of Parsons.
Courtesy of Mariwyn McClain Smith.

Parsons Centennial Committee members, 1993, *left to right, top row:* Barbara Elza, Ronda Roy, Rosemarie Davis; *bottom row:* Patricia Michael, co-chair; Jane H. Barb, co-chair; Nancy Parsons and Mary Moore.
Courtesy of Jane H. Barb.

City of Parsons Mayor and Council, 1993, *left to right, back row:* Charles "Pete"Filler, Curtis Wimer, Sam Blosser, Robert Hebb, and Pat Gray; *front row:* Mary Moore, recorder; Earl "Mutt" Delaney, mayor; and Frankie Whobrey.
Courtesy of Jane H. Barb.

Sarah Mullennex Minear, 1993.
Courtesy of Mariwyn McClain Smith.

St. George, West Virginia

At the same time Thomas Jefferson's pen was gliding over the parchment of the Declaration of Independence in far-off Philadelphia: a pioneer's axe was shaping a log in the wilderness where Saint George stands. Both came into existence that same year of 1776; Saint George in the spring, at planting time, so that a harvest could be had for the winter.[5]

St. George Courthouse, built 1858. Photo taken around 1893. *Left to right:* Cyrus Maxwell, 1863-1943, A.B. Parsons, 1843-1909, W.B. Maxwell, 1853-1926, Adam Harper Wamsley, 1838-1903, Luke Gregory Bonnifield, 1882-1949, Arnold Allen Henry Bonnifield, 1845-1936, Will Edgar Cupp, 1856-1933, Lloyd Hansford, 1857-1916, Creed Wilbur Minear, 1868-1946, Lorenza Sidney Auvil, 1853-1924, William M. Cayton, 1862-1909, George Francis Griffith, 1856-1930, Henry W. Dumire, 1861-1948. *Courtesy of Jane H. Barb.*

[5] *History of Tucker County*, Homer Floyd Fansler, 1962, fourth printing 1998, McClain Printing Company, Parsons, WV.

St. George Courthouse -- Records were removed in 1893 to take to Parsons.
Courtesy of Jane Pifer.

St. George, 1904. Minear & Mitchell
(John W. Minear and Albert Mitchell).
Courtesy of Chris Kidwell.

1913 postcard.
Courtesy of Chris Kidwell.

St. George Courthouse.
Courtesy of Jane Pifer.

The Minear family first came to Tucker County (then Randolph County) in 1774. John Minear came with a group of men and built Fort Minear, a small blockhouse at "the horseshoe" on Cheat River. The St. George courthouse was built later on the lot. The log home was replaced years later (circa 1875-1880) with the farmhouse shown here. This land still belongs to the Minear family.
Courtesy of Jane Pifer.

143

John Adams' house. It is believed that John Adams built this house in 1870, for his new wife, Angelica. The Adams' house was the first of the four up-right houses built in St. George by Daniel L. Dumire, a master carpenter of his time. He lived from 1831-1913. Dumire helped build the St. George Methodist Church known as the "Anna Eliza" Church at that time. He also built the Methodist Episcopal Church South in St. George in 1859 which sat at the lower end of town near the courthouse.
Courtesy of Jane Pifer.

Monument to Jonathan Minear. "During an Indian attack on Fort Minear at Saint George in 1781 Jonathan Minear returned to his farm to feed his livestock and was surprised and killed by Indians at this site."
Courtesy of Jane Pifer.

U.S. Post Office at St. George, postcard.
Courtesy of Chris Kidwell.

A close-up photo of the old St. George Courthouse, long after the records were moved to Parsons. Fred Barr is one of the boys pictured.
Courtesy of Chris Kidwell.

Enterprise Hotel, first in St. George, 1892.
Courtesy of Jane H. Barb.

St. George Academy.
Courtesy of Jane H. Pifer.

St. George Academy – Built 1885-86

The first move toward higher education in Tucker County was in 1885, when an Academy was started in St. George. It was done entirely by private capital through the efforts of John J. Adams, Rufus Maxwell, Wilson H. Maxwell, Dr. Bascom Baker, Silas Newton Swisher, Philetus Lipscomb and W.M. Talbott.

READ

ECHOES OF THE PAST

By HOMER FLOYD FANSLER

A series of historical and biographical items published periodically in THE PARSONS ADVOCATE.

St. George Bridge, postcard.
Courtesy of Chris Kidwell.

School at Leadmine, 1937-1938. *Front row seated:* Robert Young, Leon Kelly, Clifford Stahl and Donald Kight; *front row standing*: Delores Stahl (visiting child), Arvella Auvil, Marion Nestor, Georgia Watring, Jean Young, Wilda Fansler, Doris Harper, Loueda Auvil, Annabelle Kight, and Evelyn Hebb; *back row:* Gerald Stahl, Verla Lipscomb, Naomi Evans, Frances Maish (teacher), Layla Kight, Sybil Rummel, Ivan McCue and Robert Watring.
Courtesy of Evelyn Chaney.

The farmer Mt. Prospect School, photographed in 2007.
Courtesy of Ray and Lucille Adams.

St. George Ball Team, circa 1907.
Courtesy of Chris Kidwell.

TRUSTEES were appointed to schools in Tucker County in the early 1900s and Warner Ashby, who held that position, was visiting the Mt. Prospect School when this photo was taken about 1912. Mr. Ashby, *back left.* Seen next to him are John Harsh, Tony Dumire, and Floyd Harsh. *In the center row, left to right*: Carrie Calvert, Burton Harsh, Della Adams Dumire, Albert Adams, and Jim Beavers. *Front row*: Ted Dumire, Eva Adams, Arthur Harsh, Mabel Harsh, Clarence Harsh, Selby Adams, Dave Gainer, teacher. Photo supplied by Ted Dumire.
Courtesy of Ray and Lucille Adams.

Log home of Daniel Kaylor Dumire (b. 1830 or 1831, d. 1897). Thought to be built before the Civil War.
Courtesy of Jane Pifer.

Lena Lipscomb, Baby Susie, Rose, Tom and Elza Barr, Barr's Esso Station and Garage, St. George.
Courtesy of Chris Kidwell.

Hickory Grove School (one-room), near Hile Run between Leadmine and St. George, 1933. Standing, *left to right:* Hervey Helbig, Gilbert Wiles, Mary Hebb (eighth grade), Mrs. Mary Lea Lambert, teacher, Velva Lipscomb (seventh grade), Everett Wiles, and Robert Helbig; *kneeling:* Lena Lipscomb and Holly Helbig.
Courtesy of Evelyn Chaney.

1913, postcard.
Courtesy of Chris Kidwell.

St. George School, eighth grade class, 1943. *Left to right:* Jean Sturm, Catherine Kyle, Wesley Cassidy, Grace Lipscomb, James Jones and Evelyn Hebb.
Courtesy of Evelyn Chaney.

One-room school at St. George.
Courtesy of Jane Pifer.

Dottie White, school teacher and piano teacher at United Methodist Church in St. George.
Courtesy of Jane Pifer.

Joyce Hebb and Delain Bohon (Mullenax).
Courtesy of Delain Mullenax.

_____ and Michael Harsh, last days of Mt. Olivet School, August 15, 1970.
Courtesy of Ray and Lucille Adams.

Students at St. George School, April 23, 1929. B.R Meadows and Clara Ball, teachers.
Courtesy of Jane Pifer.

Students at St. George School, B.R. Meadows and Clara Ball, teachers.
Courtesy of Jane Pifer.

Photo of the entire student body of Number 5 School on Licking Creek Road for grades one through eight circa 1942-1945. The school is no longer standing due to damage from a tree falling on it. Most of these students went on to attend Parsons High School, in most cases riding a small bus part of the way and then transferring to a larger bus to continue on to Parsons.
Courtesy of Annetta Shahan Creekmore.

Residents of St. George.
Courtesy of Jane Pifer.

St. George.
Man *seated far left* is W. B. Jenkins.
Courtesy of Jane Pifer.

Left to right: John Barr, Dunk Close, Chet Close, Kelly Marquess and Joe Close.
Courtesy of Jane Pifer.

Bohon Family Reunion.
Far left: Tony Bohon *holding child*.
Courtesy of Delain Mullenax.

Left to right: Ally, Robert and Jessy Friend, Elizabeth Bohon, _____, Crystalena Cassidy and Janet Bohon. Seated is Hattie Miller.
Courtesy of Delain Mullenax.

Tony Bohon, *far right*.
Courtesy of Delain Mullenax.

153

Daniel L. Dumire and Susan Catherine Spessert.
Courtesy of Jane Pifer.

Harve Cassidy and Ray Jenkins.
Courtesy of Jane Pifer.

Left to right: Anna Cupp, Mildred, (doll), Eileen Hamm, Mary Jenkins and Anna Jenkins.
Courtesy of Jane Pifer.

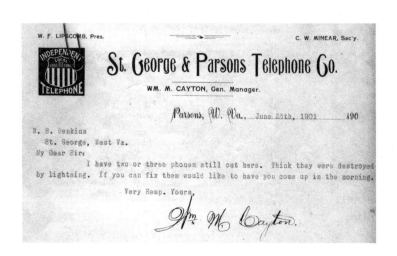

W. F. LIPSCOMB, Pres.   C. W. MINEAR, Sec'y.

St. George & Parsons Telephone Co.

WM. M. CAYTON, Gen. Manager.

Parsons, W. Va., June 25th, 1901 190

W. B. Jenkins
    St. George, West Va.
My Dear Sir:
        I have two or three phones still out here. Think they were destroyed
by lightning. If you can fix them would like to have you come up in the morning.

        Very Resp. Yours,

        Wm. M. Cayton.

154

John Jenkins
and Bradford Marquess.
Courtesy of Jane Pifer.

John Jenkins, "Bingo,"
and Duncan Close.
Courtesy of Jane Pifer.

Ray Jenkins, John Jenkins and
seated, William Jenkins.
Courtesy of Jane Pifer.

Unknown in St. George -- could possibly be casket factory at left of old St. George Bridge.
Courtesy of Jane Pifer.

J.M. Jenkins family. *Left to right*: Alverdie, Delton, Della, W.B., and Ella Jenkins, James Silas (?), and Sadie Jenkins Parsons.
Courtesy of Jane Pifer.

Unknown, St. George.
Courtesy of Jane Pifer.

Unknown, St. George.
Courtesy of Jane Pifer.

Texie Anna Hebb and Imogene Rochelle Hebb, daughters of Alva Jay and Lilly Jane Evans Hebb. Photo taken at home in St. George, summer of 1942.
Courtesy of Evelyn Chaney.

Delain Bohon (Mullenax), Tony Bohon and Betty Moreland (Knicely), Mill Run.
Courtesy of Betty Knicely.

Left to right: Anna Jenkins, Nora Dumire, Ruby Fitzwater, Frances Nestor, and, *seated*, Murl Dumire.
Courtesy of Jane Pifer.

Harve Cassidy, Elbert Dumire and Ray Jenkins.
Courtesy of Jane Pifer.

Left to right: John Jenkins, Mrs. Jenkins, Sylvester Albright, Louise Albright, George Falkenstine, Mrs. Falkenstine, Gladys Falkenstine, W.B. Jenkins, Ray Jenkins and Anna Jenkins.
Courtesy of Jane Pifer.

The Jenkins Family, *left to right*: Ray, Mrs. Mary Jenkins, Anna, John, W.B. and Anna.
Courtesy of Jane Pifer.

Family of Elliot Franklin Evans and Martha Ellen Smith Evans at homeplace farm between Leadmine and Shaffertown. *Left to right*: Elmer, Martha Ellen, Virgie Olive, Elliot Franklin, Lilly Jane, and Freeman Evans, 1914.
Courtesy of Evelyn Chaney.

Charles Austin Evans and Orpha May Evans, children of Elliot Franklin and Martha Ellen Smith Evans at home farm between Leadmine and Shaffertown, WV, 1937.
Courtesy of Evelyn Chaney.

Family of Jonah and Jane Arnold Smith. *Back row*: Maggie Bell (married Dennis Rinker, moved to Wyoming, near Kaycee), and David Wright; *front row*: Jacob Walter, Martha Ellen (married Elliot Franklin Evans), Jane, Jonah and John Andrew. They farmed the Leadmine, area, 1893.
Courtesy of Evelyn Chaney.

Alva Jay Hebb and his wife, Lilly Jane Evans Hebb at their home in St. George, 1946-1947.
Courtesy of Evelyn Chaney.

Laura Grace (Entler) Smith, wife of John Andrew Smith and children, Cleta, Elva and Maggie. The family farmed in the Leadmine area. Photo taken circa 1914-1915.
Courtesy of Evelyn Chaney.

Family of Frank and Mary Lipscomb. *Left to right:* Mary and Frank Lipscomb, Rosa Lipscomb (daughter-in-law, wife of Daniel Lipscomb) *holding grandson*, Vittie Lipscomb, Rufus Lipscomb (*in back*), Stella Lipscomb Hebb, Thomas Lipscomb, their son, Alva (*in front*), Judith Lipscomb, Dorsey and Anna Lipscomb James. Frank and Mary farmed in the Leadmine area. Photo taken circa 1913.
Courtesy of Evelyn Chaney.

Elmer and Freeman Evans, sons of Elliot Franklin Evans and Martha Ellen Smith Evans, circa 1912. The Evans farm was between Leadmine and Shaffertown. *Courtesy of Evelyn Chaney.*

David Crawford Evans and wife, Olive Calhoun Evans who farmed near Leadmine. *Courtesy of Evelyn Chaney.*

Left to right, back row: Ella and Della Jenkins; *front row:* Alverdie Jenkins, Ann C. Houston-Jenkins, (April 28, 1837 - January 9, 1918) wife of John M. Jenkins, St. George; Sadie Jenkins Parsons, wife of C.C. Parsons, b.1841, St. George. *Courtesy of Chris Kidwell.*

Thomas William Hebb and Stella Catherine Lipscomb Hebb with son, Alva Jay Hebb (born December 9, 1909, at William). Thomas worked in the coal mines and built a four-room log house on Hile Run near Leadmine. Photo February 1910. *Courtesy of Evelyn Chaney.*

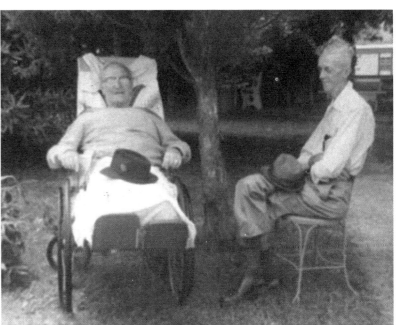

_____ and Ray Jenkins
at Jenkins' home, St. George.
Courtesy of Chris Kidwell.

Tilden VanMeter and wife, Bertha Evans
VanMeter. They farmed the Leadmine area.
Photo circa 1908.
Courtesy of Evelyn Chaney.

Carrie Dumire Calvert with dog,
St. George.
Courtesy of Chris Kidwell.

John Jenkins, St. George.
Courtesy of Chris Kidwell.

W.B. Jenkins's Home.
Courtesy of Jane Pifer.

Mr. and Mrs. W.B. Jenkins.
Courtesy of Jane Pifer.

Mrs. Mary Jenkins.
Courtesy of Jane Pifer.

Left to right: Murle Dumire, Anna Jenkins, Norah Dumire and Earl Dumire.
Courtesy of Jane Pifer.

Standing left to right: E.C. Dumire, Solomon Dumire, Nora Dumire Tenney, Murle Dumire Close; *front row*, Dennis Dumire (married to Elizabeth Auvil), and Earl Dumire, (child unknown).
Courtesy of Jane Pifer.

Mrs. Shaffer, Mrs. Jenkins, Anna Jenkins and Goldie Shafer, 1919. *Courtesy of Jane Pifer.*

Anna and Mary Jenkins.
Courtesy of Jane Pifer.

Delton S. and Maude Largent Jenkins, St. George.
Courtesy of Chris Kidwell.

The Adams' Farm.
Courtesy of Ray and Lucille Adams.

Piglets nursing from cow.
Courtesy of Ray and Lucille Adams.

Ray Adams--First 4-H Feeder calf from Tucker County taken to State 4-H Camp, Jackson's Mill.
Courtesy of Ray and Lucille Adams.

Benton Adams' Family.
Courtesy of Ray and Lucille Adams.

Benton Adams' home, now Ralph Adams'.
Courtesy of Ray and Lucille Adams.

Front row: Roy Adams, Benton Adams, Della Adams, Bessie Adams, Elsie Herrald. *Back row*: Eva Adams, Florida Adams, Selby Adams, Earl Dumire, Clarence Lansbury and Olan Herrald.
Courtesy of Ray and Lucille Adams.

George Adams' home.
Courtesy of Ray and Lucille Adams.

Lissy and Francis Adams.
Courtesy of Ray and Lucille Adams.

Lizzie Lipscomb
and Almarine.
Courtesy of Chris Kidwell.

Day of Stella Adams' marriage. Ernest, Stella, Elbert, George W. and Anziletta Adams, September 14, 1904.
Courtesy of Ray and Lucille Adams.

Elbert Adams, age 19,
(October 30, 1895 - June 21, 1921).
Courtesy of Ray and Lucille Adams.

Peter Lipscomb Family Reunion.
Courtesy of Ray and Lucille Adams.

Lissy and Francis Adams.
Courtesy of Ray and Lucille Adams.

Selby Adams and Mike Ledden.
Courtesy of Ray and Lucille Adams.

Harold and Hubert Shaffer,
sons of Harry Shaffer.
Courtesy of Ray and Lucille Adams.

Mr. and Mrs. Ernest Adams. Mrs. Adams was formerly Vivian Lipscomb, daughter of Milford and Ruth Lipscomb.
Courtesy of Ray and Lucille Adams.

Leadmine Civilian Conservation Corp Camp, circa 1930s -- where Camp Horseshoe is located today.
Courtesy of Jean H. Burns.

Pearl Adams Randolph.
Courtesy of Ray and Lucille Adams.

Zane Stiles and Jerry Pifer.
Courtesy of Ray and Lucille Adams.

Muriel, Pearl and Eula Adams.
Courtesy of Ray and Lucille Adams.

Farming for Better Living -- Ken McClain, Ronald and Vera Knotts, Ray and Lucille Adams
with Donald Adams, and Mr. and Mrs. Granville Good.
Courtesy of Ray and Lucille Adams.

Maclellan Adams, born May 27, 1862.
Courtesy of Ray and Lucille Adams.

Mary Katherine Bonniefield Swisher, 95, teacher, Horseshoe Run and Alum Hill, (March 3, 1826 - March 13, 1921).
Courtesy of Ray and Lucille Adams.

Neva Frances Adams,
born August 31, 1917.
Courtesy of Ray and Lucille Adams.

David M. and Mary Katherine Swisher.
Courtesy of Ray and Lucille Adams.

Mack Jones,
Limestone.
Courtesy of Ray and Lucille Adams.

Unknown.
Courtesy of Ray and Lucille Adams.

A Singing School Crowd--Taken at White Ridge, Mt. Carmel Church, early 1900s most likely from 1903 to 1906. *Back row standing, left to right:* Howard Dennison, another Mr. Dennison, possibly Jerry. Arthur Dumire...Russell White...Silas Miller, A.L. Dumire... *Lady standing sideways...?* Jep Dumire, Ernest Adams and Russell Lipscomb. *Next row: face with hat in back....?* Ernest Miller, and Joe Sanders. *Sitting,* Jackie Adams, Dove Adams , *lady standing side view...?* Lula Dumire, Vivian Lipscomb, Kate Dumire, Lizzie Kisner (granddaughter of Mary Ann (James) White, Dessie Adams, Effie Dennison and Ethel Miller. *Front row,* three girls; Meril White, Dove White, Villa Wotring (later Mrs. Oliver Miller) Ettie Adams, Annie Dumire, Lizzie Lipscomb, and last ...? *Sitting in chair* is Jasper Dumire, the instructor. Usual method of these schools was for each pupil to pay a dollar and have a "meeting" about every evening for two weeks.
Courtesy of Ray and Lucille Adams.

1880s cabinet photo of J.M. Jenkins' sons from St. George. *Standing, left to right:* Frank Jenkins and James Silas Jenkins; *seated*, W.B. Jenkins and Delbert S. Jenkins.
Courtesy of Chris Kidwell.

Sadie Jenkins Parsons, daughter of J.M. Jenkins and son, Boyd M. or Delton Parsons of St. George. Wife of C.L. Parsons.
Courtesy of Chris Kidwell.

Jenny Helmick Jenkins, wife of Ray Jenkins, St. George.
Courtesy of Chris Kidwell.

St. George gang having a picnic. *Left to right:* Miss Harman, Anna Jenkins, Maurice Parsons, John Jenkins, Mary Jenkins, Ray Williams, Clyde Parsons, Dayton Williams, Jessie Williams, Minnie Pifer, Gale Shafer, and Effie Williams.
Courtesy of Chris Kidwell.

Children of Emanuel and Martha Weaver Lipscomb on a hayride, St. George, circa 1910.
Courtesy of Don Barr.

Ray Jenkins, St. George,
with his six-legged pig.
Courtesy of Chris Kidwell.

St. George, *left to right:* Glenn Judy, Fanny Bland (Pennington), Robert Thompson and Nora Tena Judy (Thompson) 1885-1957. Nora and Glenn are the children of McClellan and Annie C. Tingler Judy. Fanny is the daughter of Austin Bland and Nora T. Judy (Thompson).
Courtesy of Chris Kidwell.

United
Sept. 6th.
1855

John M. Jenkins, Feb. 3, 1831-March 12, 1901 and Ann C. Houston, April 28, 1837- Jan. 9, 1918; married Sept. 6, 1855 by Reverend Stoneroad. They arrived in St. George in 1874. Of Welch and Irish descent, they had nine children: William B., Sadie, Silas, Frank, Ella, Della, Alverdie, Dessie and Delton S.
Courtesy of Chris Kidwell.

View of St. George, circa 1880s-1890s. Photo taken across Cheat River.
Courtesy of Chris Kidwell.

SOUVENIR

MT. HOPE SCHOOL

TUCKER COUNTY WEST VIRGINIA

NOVEMBER 25, 1901--APRIL 12, 1902

Presented By

Clyde M. White,
Teacher

SCHOOL OFFICERS

W. S. Denison   H. W. Dumire
A. L. Harsh

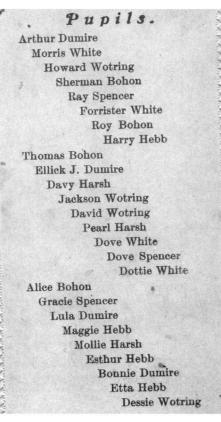

Pupils.

Arthur Dumire
Morris White
Howard Wotring
Sherman Bohon
Ray Spencer
Forrister White
Roy Bohon
Harry Hebb
Thomas Bohon
Ellick J. Dumire
Davy Harsh
Jackson Wotring
David Wotring
Pearl Harsh
Dove White
Dove Spencer
Dottie White
Alice Bohon
Gracie Spencer
Lula Dumire
Maggie Hebb
Mollie Harsh
Esthur Hebb
Bonnie Dumire
Etta Hebb
Dessie Wotring

Matilda "Tildy" Lipscomb, daughter of George and Elizabeth Lipscomb, St. George.
Courtesy of Don Barr.
St. George.
Courtesy of Chris Kidwell.

173

Big Sycamore, 1954, at Bill Minear's Sawmill on Mill Run, St. George.
Left to right: John Barr, Mel Lowther, Bill Minear, Junior Barr, Earl Taylor and Donald Barr.
Courtesy of Don Earr.

Largest tree ever cut in West Virginia. Cut in Thunderstruck near Leadmine near St. George. *Courtesy of Jane Pifer.*

Logging Crew near Leadmine.
Courtesy of Jane Pifer.

Cheat River Bridge, St. George.
Courtesy of Jane H. Barb.

David M.C. Keller, St. George.
Courtesy of Jane Pifer.

Left to right: Obie Bohon, Jesse Dickson, _____, and Howard Bohon.
Courtesy of Jane Pifer.

Logging Crew near St. George.
Courtesy of Jane Pifer.

Kerr's Camp, Mill Run.
Courtesy of Jane Pifer.

"The Merry Sawyers."
Courtesy of Jane Pifer.

River behind Shaffer House.
Courtesy of Ray and Lucille Adams.

Elmer and Lena Sturms, owners of store
and gasoline station in St. George.
Courtesy of Jane Pifer.

Emanuel Lipscomb, (December 9, 1858, St.
George - 1941). Martha Alice (Weaver) Lip-
scomb, (December 29, 1867, St. George - 1943).
Married 1884. Photo circa 1918.
Courtesy of Ray and Lucille Adams.

Richard Dumire,
July 1, 1952.
Courtesy of Ray and Lucille Adams.

Crystalena Miller Cassidy and Elizabeth Miller Bohon, twins,
celebrating their ninetieth birthdays, July 5, 2000.
Courtesy of Delain Mullenax.

Charlotte and Elmer Lipscomb, Elmer Lipcomb's General Store and Hardware,
St. George. The Lipcombs had two sons, Hollis and Keith.
Courtesy of Chris Kidwell.

Home of attorney Lloyd Hansford family, 1893, St. George. Mary Wamsley Hansford, *standing*,
and Lloyd Hansford *sitting* on the porch.
Courtesy of Jane H. Barb.

Unidentified (possibly Harsh family).
Courtesy of Ray and Lucille Adams.

Wesley Cassidy, 2001.
Courtesy of Delain Mullenax.

Carl Spessert, in front of Frank and Mildred Pifer's.
Courtesy of Ray and Lucille Adams.

Grace Taylor, Leli Simmons-Nestor and
Joann Stiles. Lelan Simmons *in front*.
Courtesy of Ray and Lucille Adams.

Hubert, Helen and
Harold Shaffer.
*Courtesy of
Ray and Lucille Adams.*

Harry and Stella Shaffer
on their wedding day.
Courtesy of Ray and Lucille Adams.

Henry St. George Tucker

The District of West Augusta, comprising the territory between the Allegheny Mountains and the Ohio River, was established in 1772. In 1776 it was divided into three Counties: Ohio, Youghiogheny and Monongalia. Acts of the Virginia Assembly created Harrison County from Monongalia in 1784, Randolph County from Harrison in 1787, and on March 7, 1856 Tucker County was formed from Randolph with County Seat at St. George. Tucker County was named for Henry St. George Tucker, Sr. (1780-1848), a Virginia jurist and law professor. The first County Seat of St. George was named for his son, Henry St. George Tucker, Jr. (1828-1863), a Confederate officer and lawyer. The second County Seat of Parsons was named for Ward Parsons, (1827-1897), planter and stockman.

St. George Methodist Church, 1930.
Courtesy of Jane Pifer.

St. George United Methodist Church,
Fall 1989.
Courtesy of Jane Pifer.

Church invitation for Easter Service.
Courtesy of Jane Pifer.

A group of people attending the St. George Methodist Church.
Courtesy of Jane Pifer.

A group of people attending the dedication of the memorial plaque
in front of the St. George Methodist Church, May 18, 1942.
Courtesy of Jane Pifer.

A group of people attending the dedication of the memorial plaque in front of the
Methodist church, May 18, 1942.
Courtesy of Jane Pifer.

Methodist Youth Group in St. George,
after an Easter sunrise service and
breakfast at Walter Jones' home, 1947.
Left to right: Evelyn Hebb, Bill Jones,
Kenneth Barr, Jim Jones, Carl Casto, Jim
Miller, and Walter (Casey) Jones, youth
director.
Courtesy of Evelyn Chaney.

Methodist Youth Group after an Easter
play practice, St. George, 1947. *Front
row:* Bill Jones, Beulah Hebb, Jean
Sturm, Robert White, Evelyn Hebb
and Jim Jones. *Back row:* Irene Dumire,
Betty Metz, Joyce Hebb, Ray Dumire
and Jim Miller.
Courtesy of Evelyn Chaney.

In front of St. George Methodist Church, 1927.
Courtesy of Jane Pifer.

This deed made the seventeenth day of November in the year of Our Lord, One Thousand Eight Hundred and Sixty-eight, Between Solomon Parsons, of Portland, Preston County, State of West Virginia of the first part, and Sansom E. Parsons - Jacob Dumire - Enoch Minear - Andrew Pifer and D.K. Dumire, of Tucker County and state aforesaid, trustees of the M.E. Church at George of the second part. Witnesseth: that in consideration of the sum of one dollar the receipt of which is herby acknowledged, the said part of the first part, do grant unto the said parties of the second part the following described property, that is to say, one piece or parcel of land. lying above or N.W. of town lots, as laid out East of Mill Run on the land of Dr. Solomon Parsons, and recorded in deed book no. -1 page 90 as part of said lots in town of St. George. Beginning at on point at said town lots and running a straight line, from the line of said lots ten feet below the church (that is erected and known as the "Annaliza" M.E. Church) to Mill Run thence with the meandering of said run to the "Old Mill Run Road" that crosses said run - thence with said road to the N. line or upper line, to the point of the above mentioned lots. Thence with said N. line or upper line to the point above mentioned, or beginning point. (Running a straight line from the upper line of said town lots, to Mill Run, being ten feet below or West of said church). And the parties of the first part, hereby convey the Said piece or parcel of land to the parties of the second part, as trustees of said church and to their successors. And the said party of the first part, do hereby covenant with the Said Parties of the Second part, that, he will warrant and defend generally the property conveyed.

Witness the following signature and seal:

Solomon Parsons

Witnessed and recorded
on November 20, 1869.

Know all men by there presence that I Solomon Parsons of the County of Randolph and State of Virginia, Lease the Annaliza Church at the mouth of "Mill Run" unto Wm. Erwin, James W. Parsons, Jonathan M. Parsons, Enoch Minear and Jacob Dumire, Trustees in trust, and their successors for the use of the Methodist Episcopal Church, to have, hold and enjoy all the rights and privileges. And have free and full and peaceful possession of Said Church, with the same rights and privileges that is given to trustees in the discipline of the Methodist Episcopal Church the same as though it was deeded. So long as it is used by the Methodist Episcopal Church as a regular preaching place. And should they, the Methodist Episcopal Church, cease to use it as a place to regularly preach in, then and not until then, this lease shall be null and void and the Said Church returns to me and my heirs. In witness I set my hand and affix my seal this 15 day of December 1844.

Solomon Parsons

State of West Virginia:

On this 17th day of May 1866 This lease was produced to me John J. Adams, Recorder, within and for the county of Tucker in my office and admitted to record.

J.J. Adams, Recorder.

Deed for United Methodist Church, St. George.
Courtesy of Jane Pifer.

First St. George Church Parsonage, located where Judy Parsons's house is in 2011.
Courtesy of Jane Pifer.

Original altar and podium.
Built by Parsons' family, 1850s.
Courtesy of Jane Pifer.

Church pews built in 1954 by Woodrow Nestor (1914-1990).
Courtesy of Jane Pifer.

Gladys Jane Pifer and Charlotte Parsons,
St. George Days, 1990.
Courtesy of Jane Pifer.

Limestone United Methodist Church Christmas play.
Courtesy of Ray and Lucille Adams.

Tom and Joe Pifer, August 1955, St. George.
Courtesy of Chris Kidwell.

1920s, Nettie Lantz, wife of Price Lantz, milking a Guernsey cow, St. George.
Courtesy of Chris Kidwell.

St. George Traction and Sawdust Company.
Courtesy of Jane Pifer.

Leadmine White Oak;
cutting fire wood for log engine.
Courtesy of Chris Kidwell.

Believed to be old iron bridge across Horseshoe Run
between St. George and Limestone.
Courtesy of Chris Kidwell.

View of Limestone Mountain from
Hannahsville, February 8, 1908.
Courtesy of Chris Kidwell.

Hambleton, West Virginia

The place where the Town of Hambleton stands has been known by a myriad of names since its history began in 1783. In succession it has been named Rush's, Goff's, Goff Town, Black Fork, Hulings and Hambleton. . . .The first settler in Hambleton was John Rush, who came with his wife Eva about the year 1796, and erected a huge two-story log house on the corner of Sixth Street and the Old County Road. He owned several slaves and erected huts about the premises for them to live in. . . .[6]

Olger Falls, Hambleton, postcard, 1912.
Courtesy of Chris Kidwell.

[6] *History of Tucker County*, Homer Floyd Fansler, 1962, fourth printing 1998, McClain Printing Company, Parsons, WV.

Hambleton --
Courtesy of Bill and Retha Bilby.

Route 72 joins Seneca Trail near Hambleton, postcard. Notice the direction of the road before the Hambleton intersection prior to the way it is today.
Courtesy of Chris Kidwell.

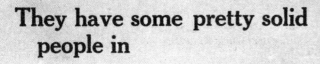

They have some pretty solid people in

HAMBLETON, W. VA.

It's a prosperous town

Postcards.
Courtesy of Chris Kidwell.

☐ 1912

Am taking a flying trip to Hambleton...

COPYRIGHT 1905. BY HOME LIFE PUBLISHING CO., N.Y.   21

Hambleton, W. Va.
830.

Greetings from
Hambleton, W.Va.

Postcards.
Courtesy of Chris Kidwell.

Main Street, Hambleton.
Courtesy of David and Rita Roberts.

Greetings from Hambleton, 1908, postcard.
Courtesy of Chris Kidwell.

PORTER'S FALLS OF HAMBLETON, W. VA.
J. IRONS & CO., PUBLISHERS

Porter's Falls of Hambleton, postcard.
Courtesy of Chris Kidwell.

ELK LICK BRIDGE, HAMBLETON, W. VA.   10

Elk Lick Bridge, Hambleton. Washed out during flood of 1954. Lies on the bottom of Blackfork River at the mouth of Elk Lick. Can be seen when water is low.
Courtesy of Chris Kidwell.

Swearingen family home, Hambleton, postcard. *Left to right:* Fannie Baker, McKinley, Charles W., Marie (Degler), Arthur and Elizabeth.
Courtesy of Chris Kidwell.

Souvenier of Hambleton Home Coming

Goff family home -- oldest house in Hambleton, 128 years, postcard.
Courtesy of Chris Kidwell.

Hambleton Lodge Badge.
Courtesy of Chris Kidwell.

Moose Home, Hambleton, postcard.
Courtesy of Chris Kidwell.

Left: Arthur Swearingen, Hambleton, postcard.
Courtesy of Chris Kidwell.

Popular doctor in Hambleton, Hendricks, and Dry Fork areas, Noah Harper Judy (1855 - June 12, 1922). Son of Martin and Christena Judy of Judy Gap. Dr. Judy was killed by a self-inflicted gunshot wound to the head with a suicide note in his pocket.
Courtesy of Chris Kidwell.

Dooley Square, Hambleton, postcard, 1911.
Courtesy of Chris Kidwell.

Sixth Street, looking east,
Hambleton, postcard, 1910.
Courtesy of Chris Kidwell.

Street Scene, Hambleton,
postcard, 1911.
Courtesy of Chris Kidwell.

Pennington Family, Hambleton, 1908.
Courtesy of Chris Kidwell.

Millie and Guy Bilby,
Hambleton, postcard.
Courtesy of Chris Kidwell.

Hambleton, *left to right*: Swearingens -- Albert, Arthur, McKinley, Elizabeth,
Marie Swearingen Degler, Fannie Baker and Charles Wesley.
Courtesy of Chris Kidwell.

Public School Building,
Hambleton, 1910.
Courtesy of Chris Kidwell.

Hambleton School,
April 1914.
Courtesy of Chris Kidwell.

Hambleton,
1915, postcard.
Courtesy of Chris Kidwell.

M.P. Church, Hambleton, 1908.
Courtesy of Chris Kidwell.

1912 Hambleton.
Courtesy of Chris Kidwell.

Presbyterian Church,
Hambleton, 1910.
Courtesy of Chris Kidwell.

Baptist Church,
Hambleton, 1910.
Courtesy of Chris Kidwell.

Picnic for members of the
Baptist Church, Hambleton,
August 17, 1911, postcard.
Courtesy of Chris Kidwell.

Hotel Hambleton.
*Courtesy of
Dave and Wilda Strahin.*

Star Restaurant,
Hambleton. Dixon's
Teamsters the morning
after July 4, 1913.
*Courtesy of
Dave and Wilda Strahin.*

HOTEL AND O. C. M. CO'S STORE, HAMBLETON, W. VA.   6

SOLD BY O. C. M. CO. DRUG DPT.

☐ Hotel and Otter Creek Mercantile Co's Store,
Hambleton, 1910, postcard.
Courtesy of Chris Kidwell.

Elk Lick, Hambleton,
May 2, 1911.
Courtesy of David and Rita Roberts.

HOTEL AND O. C. M. CO'S STORE, HAMBLETON, W. VA.   4

SOLD BY O. C. M. CO., DRUG DPT.

Elklick Lumber Company's
mill, Hambleton.
Courtesy of Bill and Retha Bilby.

Julia and friends standing in front of the
Otter Creek M. Company Store, Feb. 15,
1909, postcard.
Courtesy of Chris Kidwell.

C.A. Roberts Stores and Station, Hambleton, 1923, postcard.
Courtesy of Chris Kidwell.

Hambleton, 1913, postcard.
Courtesy of Chris Kidwell.

High water, Hambleton.
Courtesy of Chris Kidwell.

World War I, unknown,
Hambleton.

Hambleton, Western Maryland Railroad Passenger Coach railroad
workers. *Fourth from left:* "Pap" M. McKinley Swearingen.
Courtesy of Chris Kidwell.

Chef F. E. Davis and his
assistants at the Moose
Dining Hall in Hambleton,
July 4, 1912.
Courtesy of Chris Kidwell.

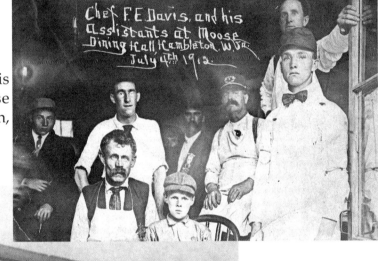

Yawkey Lumber Company, loading lumber at mill at Otter Creek.
Courtesy of Chris Kidwell.

Hambleton, July 4, 1912.
Courtesy of Chris Kidwell.

Hambleton Band, July 4, 1907. *Third person front row left to right:* William Ryan (Grace Swink's father), postcard.
Courtesy of Chris Kidwell.

"Hambleton Band on the Hike".
Courtesy of David and Rita Roberts.

Hambleton Band.
Courtesy of Chris Kidwell.

Degree of Pocahontas, Improved Order of Red Men, Hambleton, July 4, 1912, postcard.
Courtesy of Chris Kidwell.

Red Men boarding train, July 4, 1907 at Hambleton.
Courtesy of Chris Kidwell.

The Improved Order of Red Men, a fraternal organization established in Baltimore, Maryland in 1834. Their rituals and regalia are modeled after those used by Native Americans.[7]

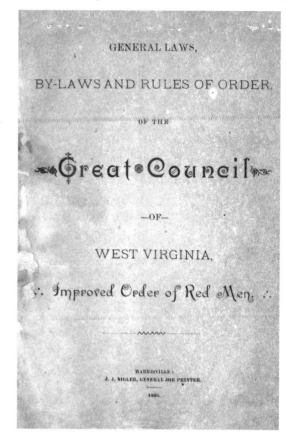
General Laws, By-Laws and Rules of Order of the Great Council of West Virginia Improved Order of Red Men.
Courtesy of Chris Kidwell.

Red Men board train from Hambleton to Davis, July 4, 1907, postcard.
Courtesy of Chris Kidwell.

Degree of Pocahontas Improved Order of Red Men, included children, Hambleton.
Courtesy of Chris Kidwell.

Royal Order of Red Men Parade, Hambleton, postcard. July 4, 1907, marching, waiting for train to Davis.
Courtesy of Chris Kidwell.

[7] http://en-wikipedia.org/wiki/Improved_Order_of_Red_Men

Hambleton, Red Men Cussewago, Tribe 90, Hambleton Cornet Band welcoming the W.V.C. & Pittsburgh Railroad. Notice the original Otter Creek Mercantile Building.
Photo Courtesy of Bruce Auvil.

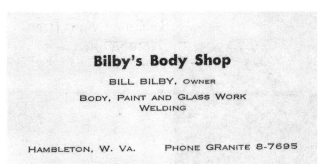

Western Maryland Water Tank
in Hambleton, at Turkey Knob.
Courtesy of Steve Bodkins.

Parade of the Red Men,
July 4, 1912, postcard.
Hambleton.
Courtesy of Chris Kidwell.

Re-enactment of Warriors
of Cussewago Tribe,
Hambleton.
Courtesy of Chris Kidwell.

Democratic Jubilee,
November 9, 1910,
Hambleton.
Courtesy of Chris Kidwell.

Hambleton-Hendricks Odd Fellows. *First person on the left (seated),* Homer Floyd Fansler; *back row, fourth person from the left,* Charles W. Swearingen.
Courtesy of Chris Kidwell.

McNeeley Cemetery, Hambleton, 1911.
Courtesy of Chris Kidwell.

Western Maryland Railroad Station, Hambleton.
Courtesy of David and Rita Roberts.

207

McKenzie Hotel burning, April 9, 1913, Hambleton, and ruins of hotel with Jeff Corrick
(Alma Corrick Mullennex's father) on wagon.
Postcards courtesy of Chris Kidwell.

Western Maryland Depot in Hambleton, 1909, postcard.
Courtesy of Chris Kidwell.

Otter Creek Mill near Hambleton.
Courtesy of Chris Kidwell.

Otter Creek Boom and Lumber Company Mill Workers,
Hambleton, postcard.
Courtesy of Chris Kidwell.

Otter Creek Boom and Lumber Company's Mill, Hambleton, postcards.
Courtesy of Chris Kidwell.

1909 postcard.

Otter Creek Mill Crew, Hambleton, 1910, postcard.

Christmas Greetings From Hambleton, W. Va.

1911 postcard.

Railroad & Lumber Docks, Otter Creek
Boom and Lumber Co.'s Mill, Hambleton.
Courtesy of Chris Kidwell.

Hauling lumber on dock, Otter
Creek, Hambleton, 1910, postcard.
Courtesy of Chris Kidwell.

Hambleton, postcard.
Courtesy of Chris Kidwell.

Caflisch Lumber Co., Hambleton, 1912, postcard.
Courtesy of Chris Kidwell.

Elklick Lumber, Hambleton.
Courtesy of Chris Kidwell.

Elk Lick Mill, Hambleton, postcard.
Courtesy of Chris Kidwell.

Hambleton.
Courtesy of Chris Kidwell.

Keystone Wood Co.'s Mill, Hambleton, postcard, 1910.
Courtesy of Chris Kidwell.

Dickson's Camp, 1909, Hambleton
on Green Mountain, postcard.
Courtesy of Chris Kidwell.

Hambleton, postcard.
Courtesy of Chris Kidwell.

Steave Fillney's Camp, 1909,
Hambleton, postcard.
Courtesy of Chris Kidwell.

This big Poplar contained 12,469
feet, Otter Creek Boom and
Lumber Co.
Courtesy of Frances Tekavec.
Submitted by Veronica Tekavec Staron.

Wreck of Engine 511, four miles
east of Hambleton, December 17,
1914; one killed, three injured.
*Courtesy of Frances Tekavec. Submitted
by Veronica Tekavec Staron.*

Green Mountain, Hambleton,
January 23, 1914, postcard.
Courtesy of Chris Kidwell.

Tannery, Hambleton.
Courtesy of Chris Kidwell.

BURNING OF THE HAMBLETON LEATHER CO'S. TANNERY.
MARCH 24TH 1910, HAMBLETON, W. VA. 3

People watching the burning of the Hambleton Leather Co.'s Tannery from McNeeley Cemetery between Hambleton and Hendricks.
Courtesy of Chris Kidwell.

Burning of the Hambleton Leather Company's Tannery, postcard, March 24, 1910, Hambleton.
Courtesy of Chris Kidwell.

BURNING OF THE HAMBLETON LEATHER CO'S. TANNERY.
MARCH 24TH 1910, HAMBLETON, W. VA. 6

BURNING OF THE HAMELETON LEATHER CO'S. TANNERY.
MARCH 24TH 1910, HAMBLETON, W. VA. 2

View of the Black Fork River showing the ruin of the Hambleton Leather Co.'s Tannery.
Courtesy of Chris Kidwell.

VIEW OF BLACK FORK RIVER SHOWING THE RUIN OF THE
HAMBLETON LEATHER CO'S TANNERY, HAMBLETON, W. VA. Mar. 1910

Ruins of the Tannery, Hambleton
Courtesy of Chris Kidwell.

1230. Ruins of The Tannery at Hambleton, W. Va.

RUIN OF THE HAMBLETON LEATHER CO'S
TANNERY, HAMBLETON, W. VA.

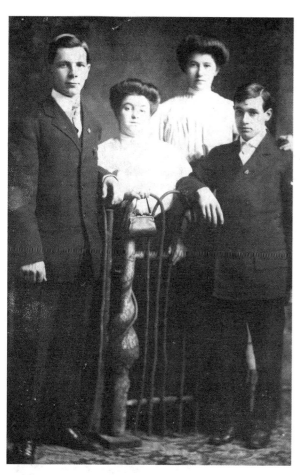

Nell Meader Family.
Courtesy of Chris Kidwell.

Meader Home, postcard.
Courtesy of Chris Kidwell.

Hambleton, 1912.
Courtesy of Chris Kidwell.

Hambleton Cubs, 1911.
Courtesy of Chris Kidwell.

Claude Luzier at bat,
Hambleton, 1914, postcard.
Courtesy of Chris Kidwell.

"The Brave Explorers," May 14, 1911, Hambleton.
Courtesy of Chris Kidwell.

Lime Rock School, 1912;
teacher, Flossie Bennett.
Courtesy of David and Rita Roberts.

Front row, left to right: Charles
Ashton Roberts, Jack, Bill and
Eugene Roberts, Lucille Eliza-
beth Haggerty Roberts and
David L. Roberts. *Back row, left
to right:* Mildred Jane, Charles,
Frederick, Benjamin and Alice
Roberts. *Courtesy of David and Rita
Roberts.*

Mildred, Charles
and Fred Roberts' home.
Courtesy of David and Rita Roberts.

Walnut Avenue,
Hambleton.
Courtesy of Chris Kidwell.

Sunday School Picnic,
Baptist Church, Hambleton,
August 17, 1911.
Courtesy of Chris Kidwell.

Logging Crew at Mackeyville. Photo taken by C.H. Palmer, photographer,
Eglon, Preston County.
Courtesy of Chris Kidwell.

Front row left to right: Shelly Mullenax (McKinnie), Craig Mullenax, Angela Nine (Nestor), Tina Richards (Hull); *second row back*: Julia Nine, held by Connie Bohon (Nestor), Crystalena Miller Cassidy, Janet Miller (Bohon) Rhoades, Howard "Buck" Rhoades, Elizabeth Miller Bohon, Glenn Mullenax and Della Bohon Akins. *Back row*: Rock Mullenax, Delain Bohon Mullenax, Robert "Bob" Bohon, Michael Mullenax, Deloris Bohon Nine, Earl Akins and Cyrus Cassidy, 1984.
Courtesy of Delain Mullenax.

Left to right: Delain Bohon Mullenax, Oved Bohon, Janet Miller (Bohon) Rhoades, Dearl Bohon, Deloris Bohon Nine, Robert "Bob" Bohon and Della Bohon Akins.
Courtesy of Delain Mullenax.

Deloris and Nick Nine, 1994.
Courtesy of Delain Mullenax.

West Virginia Governor Joe Manchin presenting the Town Council of Hambleton with a grant for town storm drains and flood control. *Left to right*: Stan Shaver, West Virginia House of Representatives, Paul Nestor and Matt Phillips, representatives of the Hambleton Town Council, Mayor of Hambleton Linda Bates, Governor Joe Manchin, Todd Schoolcraft with Michael Baker Engineering, WV Senator Bob Williams, Rosemary Wagner and Shane Whitehair, Region 7 representatives.
Courtesy of Paul Nestor.

Hendricks, West Virginia

It required one hundred years to build the Town of Hendricks. The first landowner came in 1794, and the town was incorporated in 1894. . . Henry Fansler(1761-1843) was the first settler in Hendricks. . . He built the first house in Hendricks, a log cabin on Blackwater River a mile above its confluence with Dry Fork River.[8]

Hendricks Concert Band was constantly in demand when "Tas" Mitchell was a young man. This picture, taken in front of the Old Harvey Store Building, in 1913, shows *left to right, front row*: Morton O'Neil, D. Ryan, Ralph Sherrick, Dow Huffman, J.E. Ryan, John Burger and Delpha Stemple; *middle row*: A.S. Lindsey, Russell Ward, Tas Mitchell, "Dad" Cooper, W.H. Ryan and Ice Poling; *back row*: Charlie Fisher, Bob Teter, "Dad" Miller, Harry Griffith, John Burdette and Tim Murphy.
Courtesy of Chris Kidwell.

---

[8] *History of Tucker County*, Homer Floyd Fansler, 1962, fourth printing 1998, McClain Printing Company, Parsons, WV.

A Live wire of Hendricks, postcard.
Courtesy of Chris Kidwell.

Greetings From Hendricks, 1908, postcard.
Courtesy of Chris Kidwell.

Welcome to Hendricks, postcard.
Courtesy of Chris Kidwell.

The Girls are well protected in
Hendricks, 1914, postcard.
Courtesy of Chris Kidwell.

I am taking life easy at Hendricks,
1912, postcard.
Courtesy of Chris Kidwell.

West Virginia hills as seen
above Hendricks, postcard.
Courtesy of Chris Kidwell.

On the backroad of Hendricks,
Christmas 1910, postcard.
Courtesy of Chris Kidwell.

Charles Street,
Hendricks, 1912, postcard.
Courtesy of Chris Kidwell.

Road scene Route 72, near
Hambleton and Hendricks, postcard.
Courtesy of Chris Kidwell.

Street scene, Hendricks, postcard.
Courtesy of Chris Kidwell.

Piedmont Street, Hendricks, 1910, postcard.
Courtesy of Chris Kidwell.

Street scene, Town Hill, Hendricks, postcard.
Courtesy of Chris Kidwell.

West Virginia snow scene taken by The Merchants
Photographer, Hendricks, 1912, postcard.
Courtesy of Chris Kidwell.

Street scene on Hill, Hendricks, postcard.
Courtesy of Chris Kidwell.

Home of Eugene Radcliff,
Hendricks, postcard.
Courtesy of Chris Kidwell.

Edgewood Avenue, Hendricks, postcard.
Courtesy of Chris Kidwell.

Picnic/party, July 8, 1906, Hendricks, postcard.
Courtesy of Chris Kidwell.

Home of J.E. Poling, Hendricks, postcard.
Courtesy of Chris Kidwell.

Hendricks, WV

Hendricks was incorporated in June 1894 and named for Thomas Andrew Hendricks, a vice president of the United States. The first permanent settler was Henry Fansler (1761-1843), a Revolutionary soldier, who came from Rockingham County, VA, and settled in the Canaan Valley in 1800. He moved to Hendricks in 1806 and built the first house there. Hendricks is 1,721 feet in altitude and its 1960 population was 407.

Tucker County Fair Program -- 1960.
Courtesy of Chris Kidwell.

Henry Fansler, the first permanent settler.

A Winter Scene in Hendricks, postcard.
Courtesy of Chris Kidwell.

The first house in Hendricks; built 1815, torn down 1958.

Concert band, Hendricks.
Courtesy of Chris Kidwell.

Methodist Church, Hendricks.
Courtesy of Jane H. Barb.

Methodist Church, Hendricks.
Courtesy of Jane H. Barb.

Presbyterian Church, Hendricks.
Courtesy of Jane H. Barb.

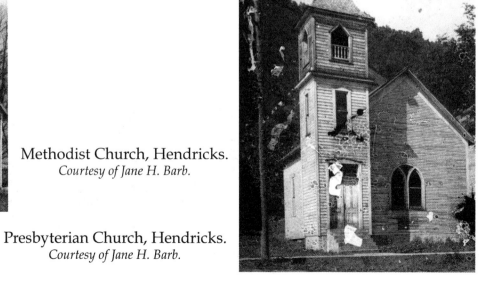

Taswell D. Mitchell, b. 1888, Hendricks. *Courtesy of Mariwyn McClain Smith from . . . and live forever, published by McClain Printing Company in 1974.*

Old abandoned lime kiln near Hendricks.
Courtesy of Chris Kidwell.

Photo taken above Hendricks' old Lime Kiln House. *Sitting on porch left to right*: Albert Lee and Arthur Lee Swearingen; *back row left to right*: Charles Wesley, Elizabeth Ann, Meredith McKinley, Fannie Bell Baker and Marie Eunice Swearingen.
Courtesy of Chris Kidwell.

T. A. LOUGHRY

1935   *Silver Anniversary*   **1960**

(Twenty-Five Years in the Same Location)

GENERAL MERCHANDISE—DRY GOODS—NOTIONS

Specializing in

RED BALL INSULATED FOOTWEAR BY BALL-BRAND

and

CHIPPEWA BOOTS & SHOES (CHIPPEWA SHOE CO.)

BIGGEST BUYER OF GINSENG IN TUCKER COUNTY

HENDRICKS, WEST VIRGINIA

Phone GR 8-4385—The Store on the Corner

T.A. Loughry ad, 1935-1960.
Courtesy of Chris Kidwell.

Post Office and Bank Building,
Hendricks, 1908, postcard.
Courtesy of Chris Kidwell.

The J.E. Poling Co. Store, postcard.
Courtesy of Chris Kidwell.

The J.E. Poling Co. Store, 1910, postcard.
Courtesy of Chris Kidwell.

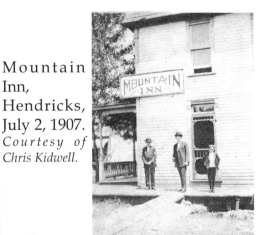

Mountain Inn, Hendricks, July 2, 1907.
Courtesy of Chris Kidwell.

Unknown woman sitting on stacked lumber at
George Davis, Charles Mullennex and Allen
Lindsey's Lumber Yard, Hendricks.
Courtesy of Chris Kidwell.

232

First National Bank, Hendricks, W. Va

First National Bank,
Hendricks, 1913, postcard.
Courtesy of Chris Kidwell.

Hendricks, W. VA., LOOKING, EAST.

Hendricks, looking east, postcard.
Courtesy of Chris Kidwell.

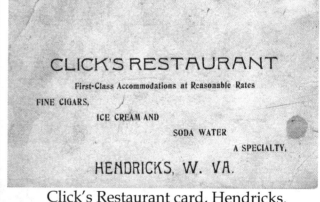

CLICK'S RESTAURANT
First-Class Accommodations at Reasonable Rates
FINE CIGARS,
ICE CREAM AND
SODA WATER
A SPECIALTY,
HENDRICKS, W. VA.

Click's Restaurant card, Hendricks.
Courtesy of Chris Kidwell.

The long, white building at the foot of the hill is the old Hendricks school (showing back of school) postcard.
Courtesy of Chris Kidwell.

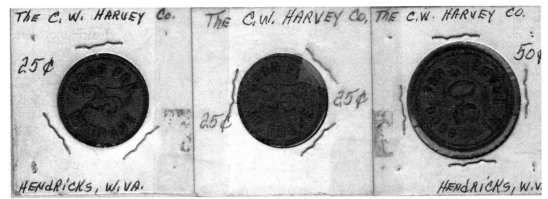

The C.W. Harvey Company's store script. *Courtesy of Chris Kidwell.*

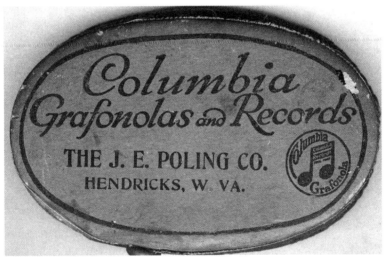

Columbia Grafonolas and Records (a brush cleaner for
old slate records) -- The J.E. Poling Co., Hendricks.
Courtesy of Chris Kidwell.

Western Maryland Railroad Engine
#38 at Hendricks, lower Blackwater
Canyon, October 8, 1972.
Courtesy of Chris Kidwell.

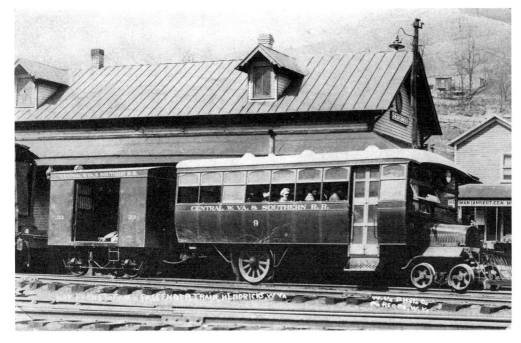

"The Jitney" for the WV Central and Southern Railroad, Dry Fork Station and Passenger Train, Hendricks, postcard.
Courtesy of Chris Kidwell.

Scene on Western Maryland Railroad between Hendricks and Thomas, postcard.
Courtesy of Chris Kidwell.

Hendricks Depot, 1908, postcard.
Courtesy of Chris Kidwell.

Hendricks Depot, postcard.
Courtesy of Chris Kidwell.

Railroad yard, Hendricks, 1906.
Courtesy of Bill and Retha Bilby.

Wreck near Hendricks,
log train, postcard.
Courtesy of Chris Kidwell.

Western Maryland Railroad.
Station, Hendricks, 1912, postcard.
Courtesy of Chris Kidwell.

Helpers on the Hendricks Grade, postcard.
Courtesy of Chris Kidwell.

Fishing on Black Fork River, Hendricks, postcard.
Courtesy of Chris Kidwell.

Hendricks, Dec. 19, 1911.
Courtesy of Chris Kidwell.

Scenery, *at the right and below,* along the Western Maryland Railroad postcard.
Courtesy of Chris Kidwell.

"Cleaning up wreckage,"
Hendricks, February 10, 1911.
Courtesy of David and Rita Roberts.

Western Maryland wreck, December 17, 1914, Big Run Curve, postcard.
Courtesy of Chris Kidwell.

WV Central Railroad
accident near Hendricks.
Courtesy of Chris Kidwell.

Freighter, Hendricks Grade, Western
Maryland Railroad, 1916, postcard.
Courtesy of Chris Kidwell.

On Hendricks Grade,
Western Maryland Railroad, 1916, postcard.
Courtesy of Chris Kidwell.

Western Maryland Railroad near the foot of
Hendricks Grade, looking south, postcard.
Courtesy of Chris Kidwell.

One of the longest locomotives in the world,
weighed 264 tons, used on the Black Fork
Grade at Hendricks, postcard.
Courtesy of Chris Kidwell.

Freighter, Hendricks Grade,
Western Maryland Railroad, 1910, postcard.
Courtesy of Chris Kidwell.

Early View of Otter Creek (Dry
Fork River) from late 1800s
steroview photo.
Courtesy of Chris Kidwell.

Big engine, used on the Hendricks Grade,
Western Maryland Railroad.
Courtesy of Chris Kidwell.

Climbing around Point
Lookout, Hendricks grade,
1911, postcard.
Courtesy of Chris Kidwell.

Western Maryland Rail-
road in front of Hendricks
Bank Building. Notice the
jeweler's clock.
Courtesy of Chris Kidwell.

Davis and Hendricks boys playing baseball, Hendricks, 1912, post-card.
Courtesy of Chris Kidwell.

Knights of Pythias Lodge III, Hendricks. Jim Ambrose *standing second from left*; Tom Hedrick *standing third from left*.
Courtesy of Jane H. Barb.

Hendricks-Hambleton Baseball Team, 1912. *Sitting left to right:* Edward Duff, Ted Gorman, Claude Luzier, W.D. Scallon, Wade Gailey and Charles Scholfield. *Standing left to right:* Sylvanus Harper, Jay Scallon, Russell Murphy, W. Ice Poling, Don Cunningham.
Courtesy of Chris Kidwell.

Hick Festival in Hendricks, 1978. *Front row, left to right:* Gertie Bodkin Judy, Isom Judy with "snuff" can; *back row:* Wade and Dessie Kidwell and Bill Judy. Paul "Koon" Sponaugle *to the right*.
Courtesy of Chris Kidwell.

Hendricks Cemetery.
Courtesy of Jane H. Barb.

Room 4, Hendricks Graded
School, Hendricks, postcard.
Courtesy of Chris Kidwell.

Public school, Hendricks.
Courtesy of Chris Kidwell.

Thought to be Mona Godwin,
Hendricks.
Courtesy of Chris Kidwell.

Road to Rosendorf, Hendricks, 1913, postcard.
Courtesy of Chris Kidwell.

Bridge at Rosendorf, postcard.
Courtesy of Chris Kidwell.

Thomas, West Virginia

Fairfax District was formed from Black Fork and Saint George Districts June 10, 1884. This was two months before the railroad came to Thomas and eight years before the town was incorporated. During that eight years the town was named "Fairfax."[9]

The third Fairfax Stone erected by the Davis Coal and Coke Company, 1885, Thomas.
Courtesy of Elmer "Slim" Moreland, submitted by Chris Kidwell.

[9] *History of Tucker County*, Homer Floyd Fansler, 1962, fourth printing 1998, McClain Printing Company, Parsons, WV.

Thomas, WV

Thomas was incorporated in August 1892 and named for Thomas Beall Davis, the Republican candidate for Governor of West Virginia, that year. It is 2,988 feet in altitude and in 1960 the population was 894. The first settler in Thomas was Jacob Christian Pase (1838-1898), who came from Clearfield County, PA, in 1880 and occupied a hunting cabin.

Jacob Christian Pase,
the first settler

Tucker County Fair Program -- 1960.
Courtesy of Chris Kidwell.

Destruction at Thomas, W. Va., by a tornado June 23, 1944

Third Street, Thomas, postcard.
Courtesy of Chris Kidwell.

Thomas.
Courtesy of Chris Kidwell.

Tipple #40, Pierce, 1896.
Courtesy of Chris Kidwell.

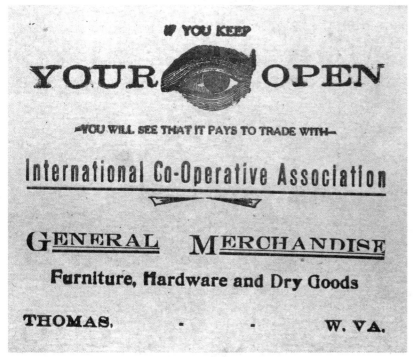

International Co-operative Association.
Courtesy of Chris Kidwell.

Thomas.
Courtesy of Chris Kidwell.

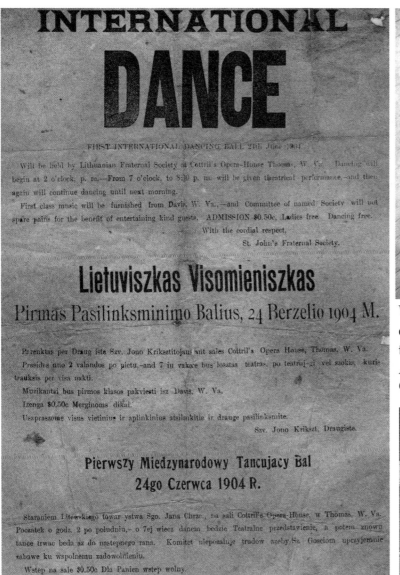

Dance poster for International People Workers around the Thomas area (in three languages), circa 1900s.
Courtesy of Chris Kidwell.

Western Maryland Railroad Express agent's office; Michael A. Getty, express agent. Pictured is Marten Higgs, assistant, Thomas, April 1902. Interior photo *below*.
Courtesy of Chris Kidwell.

Paul Meyer and Claude "George" Arnold at Meyer Exxon Station in Thomas, circa 1992. George Arnold operated the station by a hand-shake agreement with the owner, Herman A. "Jim" Meyer.
Courtesy of Susan Meyer.

Unknown, Thomas.

Thomas, 1913.
Courtesy of Chris Kidwell.

Thomas, postcard.
Courtesy of Chris Kidwell.

Front Street, Thomas,
postcard.
Courtesy of Chris Kidwell.

Thomas, postcard.
Courtesy of Chris Kidwell.

Thomas, postcard.
Courtesy of Chris Kidwell.

Thomas, 1908, postcard, horse and sleigh with bells.
Courtesy of Chris Kidwell.

Front Street, Thomas,
postcard.
Courtesy of Chris Kidwell.

Thomas, postcard.
Courtesy of Chris Kidwell.

Stephen Truman Fansler, (December 4, 1866 - July 7, 1953). Photographer in Thomas, 1892-1910.
Courtesy of Chris Kidwell.

First House in Thomas, 1860, postcard.
Courtesy of Chris Kidwell.

Skyland Lodge on Backbone Mountain, postcard. The lodge was destroyed by fire in the mid-1900s. This area became Centennial Park along U.S. Route 219.
Courtesy of Chris Kidwell.

Old Train's Inn, Route 219, postcard.
Courtesy of Chris Kidwell.

Skyland Lodge, Top of Backbone Mountain, US 219, Altitude 3,552, postcard.
Courtesy of Chris Kidwell.

Cortland Acres is a non-profit, 94-bed long-term care facility that serves people in Tucker and surrounding counties.
Courtesy of Chris Stadelman.

Early aerial photo of
Cortland Acres Nursing Home, postcard.
Courtesy of Chris Kidwell.

The newest addition to the Cortland Acres complex are The Pines, single-family homes that offer maintenance-free living with a number of additional amenities. A medical complex is due to open on the campus in 2012.
Courtesy of Chris Stadelman.

R.B. Benedetto Store front, Thomas.
Courtesy of Chris Kidwell.

Front Street, Thomas. Metropolis Hotel (men in top hats) and Miners and Merchants Bank *on right*.
Courtesy of Chris Kidwell.

Imperial Hotel,
Thomas, postcard.
Courtesy of Chris Kidwell.

SCHILANSKY & SCHATZ,

—DEALERS IN—

Clothing, Dry Goods, Notions, Boots, Shoes,

Hardware, Queensware, and General Merchandise,

Thomas, W. Va. June 25 1895

Schilansky & Schatz.
Courtesy of Chris Kidwell.

Milkints Merchantile, Charles C. Milkint & Son. Tony Milkint behind the counter,
Thomas, circa 1905-1920.
Courtesy of Chris Kidwell.

July 4, 1908, Thomas.
Courtesy of Chris Kidwell.

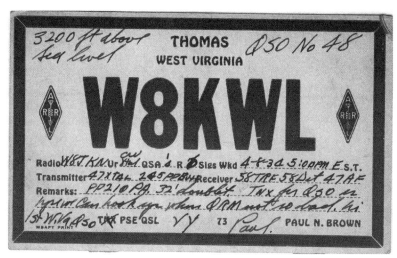

Thomas W8KWL.
Courtesy of Chris Kidwell.

Murry Building,
July 4, 1908, Thomas.
Courtesy of Chris Kidwell.

What is next? July 4, 1908, Thomas.
Courtesy of Chris Kidwell.

Hope Natural Gas Company, Smithfield.
Probably at Thomas/Davis, postcard.
Courtesy of Chris Kidwell.

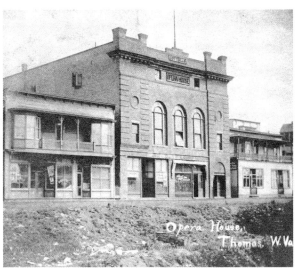

Opera House,
Thomas, 1905, postcard.
Courtesy of Ernest Arhar.

Hotel Metropolitan, Thomas, 1914, postcard.
Courtesy of Chris Kidwell.

DePollo's store, Thomas.
Courtesy of Chris Kidwell.

The Thomas Bottling Works, Thomas.
Courtesy of Chris Kidwell.

Miners' Bank and post office,
Thomas, 1909, postcard.
Courtesy of Chris Kidwell.

Unknown (possible wedding photo). Photo by
Broadwater Art Studio, Thomas.
Courtesy of Chris Kidwell.

Miners and Merchants Bank, 1926.
Courtesy of Chris Kidwell.

John Thomas Kidwell worked on this train for many years, Thomas.
Courtesy of Chris Kidwell.

Train, Thomas.
Courtesy of Chris Kidwell.

Thomas Train Depot.
Courtesy of Chris Kidwell.

Western Maryland Railroad Depot, Thomas, postcard, 1907.
Courtesy of Chris Kidwell.

The first depot at Thomas;
leaving Thomas for Parsons, postcard.
Courtesy of Chris Kidwell.

Western Maryland Railroad Station,
Thomas, postcard, 1903.
Courtesy of Chris Kidwell.

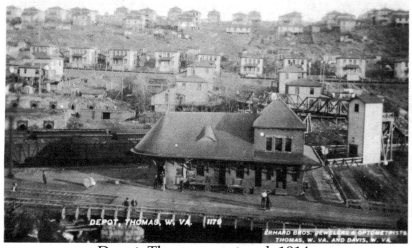

Depot, Thomas, postcard, 1914.
Courtesy of Chris Kidwell.

Table Rock Inn, top of
Backbone Mountain, Elevation 5,095.
Courtesy of Chris Kidwell.

Western Maryland Rail-
road, Thomas, postcard.
Courtesy of Chris Kidwell.

No. 1 Davis Branch at Thomas,
postcard.
Courtesy of Chris Kidwell.

Thomas.
Courtesy of Chris Kidwell.

Coke Oven, Thomas,
1911, postcard.
Courtesy of Chris Kidwell.

Wreck of Western Maryland Railroad,
Round House, Thomas, postcard.
Courtesy of Chris Kidwell.

Western Maryland
"Maud," Thomas.
Courtesy of Chris Kidwell.

Round House,
Thomas, 1911, postcard.
Courtesy of Chris Kidwell.

Round House,
Thomas, 1909, postcard.
Courtesy of Chris Kidwell.

Western Maryland Railroad.
workers at the Round House
in Thomas, postcard.
Courtesy of Chris Kidwell.

"Coal Works," Thomas, postcard.
Courtesy of Ernest Arhar.

Davis Coal and Coke Co.'s coal works, Thomas.
Courtesy of Chris Kidwell.

The Thomas Dam,
August 31, 1911,
postcard.
*Courtesy of
Chris Kidwell.*

Smoke stack, DC&C Co., Thomas.
Courtesy of Chris Kidwell.

Hoisting Engine, Mine 39, Pierce.
Courtesy of Chris Kidwell.

Shaft at Thomas, postcard.
Courtesy of Chris Kidwell.

Mine 25, Thomas, postcard.
Courtesy of Chris Kidwell.

Drivers, No. 5 Mine, Douglas.
Courtesy of Chris Kidwell.

Mine #26, June 1911, Thomas.
Courtesy of Frances Tekavec. Submitted by Veronica Tekavec Staron.

Front Street, Thomas,
1918 postcard.
Courtesy of Jane H. Barb.

Milkint's Garage, Thomas, postcard.
Destroyed in snowstorm, winter 2010-2011.
Courtesy of Chris Kidwell.

Shaft, Pierce, 1914, postcard.
Courtesy of Chris Kidwell.

Davis Coal & Coke offices, Thomas.
Courtesy of Chris Kidwell.

Thomas, postcard.
Courtesy of Chris Kidwell.

**Buxton Landstreet Co.
Building/Store, Thomas.**
Courtesy of Chris Kidwell.

1909 postcard.
Courtesy of Chris Kidwell.

A.H. Baer & Sons Men's and Ladies'
Furnishings. Stores were located in
Thomas and Parsons.

Aerial view of Thomas.
Courtesy of Mariwyn McClain Smith.

Woods-Log Camp, Blackwater
Canyon, near Douglas.
Courtesy of Chris Kidwell.

Thought to be school
children in Thomas.
Courtesy of Chris Kidwell.

Logging Tub Run Bridge, near Thomas, 1910, (notice cable and steam engine).
Courtesy of Chris Kidwell.

Logging.
Courtesy of Chris Kidwell.

Log Bucking Contest, July 4, 1910, Thomas.
Courtesy of Chris Kidwell.

Parade, July 4, Thomas.
Courtesy of Chris Kidwell.

Fireman from fire department, postcard, Thomas. *Centered in photo,* Fire Chief Slim Fansler.
Courtesy of Chris Kidwell.

Water sports, swimming pool, Thomas, postcard. Thomas Studio, photo.
Courtesy of Chris Kidwell.

Bridge and Dam at Thomas.
Courtesy of Chris Kidwell.

Front Street, Thomas, postcards.
Courtesy of Jane H. Barb.

Portion of business section,
Thomas, postcard.
Courtesy of Jane H. Barb.

A portion of the business
section of Thomas, postcard.
Courtesy of Jane H. Barb.

Thomas, postcard.
Courtesy of Jane H. Barb.

July 5, 1909 in Thomas, 1912 (stamped), postcard.
Courtesy of Jane H. Barb.

**Destruction by "cyclone,"
June 23, 1944, Thomas.**
Courtesy of Chris Kidwell.

Courtesy of Jane H. Barb.

View of Benbush, from
Mine 38, 1913, postcard.
Courtesy of Chris Kidwell.

Methodist Episcopal Church, Thomas,
1910, postcard, W.C. Strohmeyer, pastor.
Courtesy of Chris Kidwell.

Catholic Church, Thomas, postcard.
Courtesy of Chris Kidwell.

Catholic Church, Thomas, postcard.
Courtesy of Chris Kidwell.

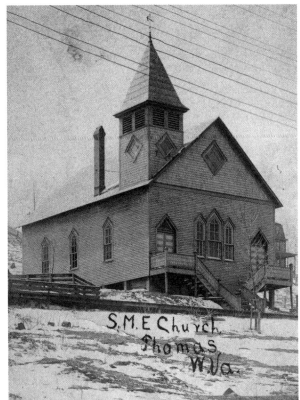

Methodist Episcopal Church,
Thomas, postcard.
Courtesy of Chris Kidwell.

Catholic Church, Thomas, postcard.
Courtesy of Jane H. Barb.

Thomas High School, postcards.

1912.

Roy Goss, (football player) 1900 US Census, Bayard, August 1890. Parents David Goss b. April 1856 and Mary E. Goss, b. April 1869. Brewner (son) born November 1894.
Courtesy of Chris Kidwell.

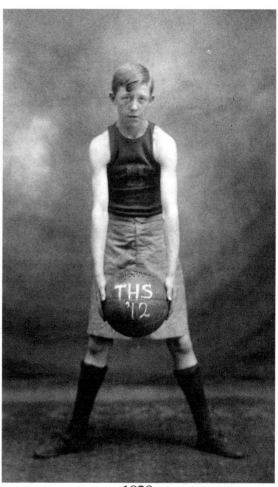

1920.

Thomas High School fullback, Tony Grigaliunas, 1922, postcard.
Courtesy of Chris Kidwell.

SUTTON THEATRE

THOMAS, WEST VIRGINIA

Program for April 1939

Show Starts Mon. 5 p.m. Other Nights 7:00 and 9	CHILD - 10c ADULT - 25c	Western Electric Microphonic Sound System

SAT. APR. 1   Double Feature- Matinee and Night   7-UP

"BOY SLAVES"
with ANN SHIRELY- ROGER DANIEL

"COME ON RANGER"
with ROY ROGERS

MON-TUES. ARR. 3-4   BANK NIGHTS

"FISHERMAN'S WARF"
with BOBBY BREEN- LEO CARILLO- HENRY ARMETTA

WED-THUR APR. 5-6   A Metro-Goldyn Mayer Picture

"THE CITADEL"
with ROBERT DONAT- ROSALIND RUSSELL
Added- "Goffy and Wilbur" Disney Cartoon

FRI. APR. 7   GIFT-A-FUR NIGHT

"KING OF THE UNDERWORLD"
with KAY FRANCIS- HUMPHREY BOGART

SAT. APR. 8   Double Feature- Matinee and Night   (7-UP)

"SMILING ALONG"
with GRACIE FIELDS

"PURPLE VIGILANTIES"
with THE THREE MESQUITEERS

MON-TUES. APR. 10-11   BANK NIGHTS

"THE GREAT MAN VOTES"
with JOHN BARRMORE- PETER HOLDEN

WED-THUR. MAR. 12-13 Metro-Goldyn Mayer Picture In Technicolor

"SWEETHEARTS"
with NELSON EDDY- JEANETTE MacDONALD

FRI. APR. 14   GIFT-A-FUR NIGHT

"INSIDE STORY"
with MICHAEL WHALEN- JEAN ROGERS

SAT. APR. 15   Double Feature- Matinee and Night   (7-UP)

"DEVIL'S ISLAND"
with BORIS KARLOFF- NEDA HARRIGAN

"THE TERROR OF TINY TOWN"
with BILLY CURTIS

MON-TUES. APR. 17-18   BANK NIGHTS

"THE RAGE OF PARIS"
with DOUGAS FAIRBANKS, JR.- DANIELLE DARRIEUX

WED-THUR. APR. 19-20   A Warner Brothers Picture

"DAWN PATROL"
with ERROL FLYNN- DAVID NIVEN

FRI. APR. 21   (7-UP)

"EVERYBODY'S BABY"
with THE JONES FAMILY

SAT. APR. 22   (Double Feature)   2:30-7:00-9:15 P. M.

"ARIZONA LEGION"
with GEORGE O'BRIEN

"TORCHY IN CHINATOWN"
with GLENDA FARRELL- BARTON MacLANE

SUTTON THEATRE

THOMAS, WEST VIRGINIA

Program for June 1939

Show Startss Mon. 5 p.m. Other Nights 7:15 & 9:15	CHILD - 10c ADULT - 25c	Western Electric Microphonic Sound System

WED-THUR. MAY 31, JUNE 1   A Return Engagement

"JESSIE JAMES"
with TYRONE POWER- NANCY KELLY- HENRY FONDA

FRI. JUNE 2   (7-UP)

"OFF THE RECORD"
with PAT O'BRIEN- JOAN BLONDELL

SAT. JUNE 3   (Double Feature)   7:00- 9:30 P. M.

"MEXICALI ROSE"
with GENE AUTRY- SMILEY BURNETTE

"MR. MOTO ON DANGER ISLAND"
with PETER LORRE- JEAN HERSHOLT

MON-TUES. JUNE 5-6   BANK NIGHTS

"YES MY DARLING DAUGHTER"
with JEFFREY LYNN- PRISCILLA LANE-
MAY ROBSON- ROBERT YOUNG

WED-THUR. JUNE 7-8   Added- March of Time and Other Shorts

"THE OKLAHOMA KID"
with JAMES CAGNEY- HUMPHREY BOGART
ROSEMARY LANE

FRI. JUNE 9   (7-UP)

"THEY MADE HER A SPY"
with SALLY EILERS- ALLEN LANE

SAT. JUNE 10   (Double Feature)   7:00-9:30 P. M.

"WINNER TAKE ALL"
with TONY MARTIN- GLORIA STUART
SLIM SUMMERVILLE- HENRY ARMETTA

"IN OLD MONTANA"
with FRED SCOTT

MON-TUES. JUNE 12-13   BANK NIGHTS

"WIFE, HUSBAND AND FRIEND"
with LORETTA YOUNG- WARNER BAXTER

WED-THUR. 14-15   Metro-Goldwyn Mayer Picture

"HONOLULU"
with ELEANOR POWELL- ROBERT YOUNG- GEORGE BURNS

FRI. JUNE 16   (7-UP)

"WOMEN IN THE WIND"
with KAY FRANCIS- WILLIAM GARGAN

SAT. JUNE 17   Return Engagement

"SAN FRANCISCO"
with CLARK GABLE- JEANETTE MacDONALD
SPENCER TRACY

MON-TUES. JUNE 19-20   BANK NIGHTS

"CALLING DR. KILDARE"
with LIONEL BARRYMORE- LEW AYRES
Added- "Donald's Cousin Gus," a Disney Cartoon"

WED-THUR. JUNE 21-22   The Academy Award Winner

"YOU CAN'T TAKE IT WITH YOU"
with JEAN ARTHUR- JAMES STUART
LIONEL BARRYMORE- EDWARD ARNOLD

Sutton Theatre, Thomas, April and June 1939, programs.
Courtesy of Chris Kidwell.

West Coketon School, 1912, Geo. Paugh, teacher, 1912, postcard.
Courtesy of Chris Kidwell.

Coketon Schools, 1915, postcard.
Courtesy of Chris Kidwell.

Frank J. Fisher, Coketon, from 1910 WV census. Hellena Fisher (mother), John and Frank (sons), Anna, Katie and Hellena (daughters). Served in World War I; killed in action October 19, 1918.
Courtesy of Chris Kidwell.

Coketon, an unincorporated community in Tucker County, lies at the confluence of Snyder Run and the North Fork Blackwater River south of the town of Thomas.

In the 1880s and 1890s, former Senator Henry Gassaway Davis's Davis Coal and Coke Company, worked over one thousand coke ovens and nine coal mines within one mile of their central office at Coketon. [10]

[10] http://en.wikipedia.org/wiki/Unincorporated_community

Coketon, population in 1920
was 300, postcard.
Courtesy of Ernest Arhar.

View of Pierce, 1912, postcard.
Courtesy of Chris Kidwell.

Pierce, opera house,
postcard.
Courtesy of Chris Kidwell.

Pierce, *left to right*, third building is
the opera house, postcard.
Courtesy of Chris Kidwell.

Pierce.
Courtesy of Veronica Tekavec Staron.

Pierce.
Courtesy of Veronica Tekavec Staron.

Work crew cutting clearing for Pierce, (thought to be Mine #43), circa
1912-1914. *Left to right*: Thomas William Hebb, Mr. Henry Tasker *(with an
ax on his shoulder)*, mine representative. *Front row, extreme right:* Nelson
Jones, son of Simon and Sue Jones who owned the farm on Hile Run.
Courtesy of Evelyn Chaney.

"Greetings from Albert" --
Albert was the post office name
for Douglas.
Courtesy of Chris Kidwell.

Douglas, postcard.
Courtesy of Chris Kidwell.

Douglas, 1909, postcard.
Courtesy of Chris Kidwell.

Douglas Falls, Seneca
Trail, Thomas, postcard.
Courtesy of Chris Kidwell.

Douglas.
Courtesy of Chris Kidwell.

VIEW OF WILLIAM, W. VA., SHOWING MILL DAM.   14

View of William, showing
mill dam, 1910 postcard.
Courtesy of Chris Kidwell.

William, 1905.
Courtesy of Chris Kidwell.

Ready for R. Chaffey's Annual picnic, William, 1911, postcard.
Courtesy of Chris Kidwell.

Rhubarbs (suburbs) of William.
Courtesy of Chris Kidwell.

Three views of burning of Chaffey's Mill, William, June 25, 1907, postcard.
Courtesy of Chris Kidwell.

Chaffey's New Mill,
William, postcard.
Courtesy of Chris Kidwell.

North Fork of Blackwater
near Douglas, 1912, postcard.
Courtesy of Chris Kidwell.

Handle Factory,
William, 1909, postcard.
Courtesy of Chris Kidwell.

Rescue party at No. 20 Mine disaster, April 24, 1911,
at Elk Garden, at the foot of the mountain.
Courtesy of Chris Kidwell.

Davis, West Virginia

The Town of Davis was conceived in the mind of Henry Gassaway Davis as early as March 27, 1871, but he was undecided just where to locate it until Christmas Day 1882. Between March 27, 1871, and June 18, 1873, Davis and his brothers, Thomas B., and William R., purchased six tracts of land, containing 23,550 acres, in what is now Fairfax and Davis districts of Tucker County, paying $13,355.00 for them which amounted to 57 cents an acre.[11]

Blackwater Falls.
Courtesy of Frances Tekavec.
Submitted by Veronica Tekavec Staron.

[11] *History of Tucker County*, Homer Floyd Fansler, 1962, fourth printing 1998, McClain Printing Company, Parsons, WV.

Welcome to Davis, 1933, postcard.
Courtesy of Chris Kidwell.

Blackwater Falls,
early 1900s.
*Courtesy of Chris
Kidwell.*

At Blackwater Falls, Davis, (arrow indicates a girl diving from Falls), postcard.
Courtesy of Chris Kidwell.

Winter view, Blackwater Falls, postcard.
Courtesy of Chris Kidwell.

Scene at Blackwater Falls, Davis, postcard.
Courtesy of Jane H. Barb.

Early Davis, 1885.
Courtesy of Chris Kidwell.

Early view of Blackwater Falls, 1980s.
Courtesy of Chris Kidwell.

Views of the Blackwater River, three miles
above Davis, 1907, postcard.
Courtesy of Chris Kidwell.

John Raese's House, Davis, 1886, postcard.
Courtesy of Chris Kidwell.

Blackwater Falls, postcard.
Courtesy of Chris Kidwell.

Above the Blackwater Falls,
Davis, postcard.
Courtesy of Chris Kidwell.

Blackwater River above Blackwater Falls, Davis, 1900s.
Family outing/picnic, Albert McCleary *standing second from left.*
Courtesy of Chris Kidwell.

Fishing below Blackwater Falls,
Davis, postcard.
Courtesy of Chris Kidwell.

Blackwater Falls
in the wintertime, postcard.
Courtesy of Chris Kidwell.

Blackwater Falls standing platform, postcard.
Courtesy of Chris Kidwell.

The Rotunda of Blackwater Falls,
postcard.
Courtesy of Chris Kidwell.

Blackwater Canyon seen from Canyon Point, postcards.
Courtesy of Chris Kidwell.

West Virginia Pulp and Paper Co. Pulp Mill, Davis, postcard, July 11, 1909. One of the ladies is Viola McMahon Ingram Clark (1884-1918). The gentleman is Patrick C. Clark (1877-1966). Viola was the daughter of Albert and Catherine Ingram, Davis. *Courtesy of Chris Kidwell.*

Bridge at Blackwater River.
Courtesy of Chris Kidwell.

Blackwater Canyon showing railroad, Davis, 1915, postcard.
Courtesy of Chris Kidwell.

View over Canaan Valley near Davis,
altitude over 3,000 feet, 1944, postcard.
Courtesy of Chris Kidwell.

View of Canaan Valley.
Courtesy of Chris Kidwell.

Davis, 1909, postcard;
hemlock bark.
Courtesy of Chris Kidwell.

Bald Knob -- 4,315 feet high, seen
from Canaan Valley, postcard.
Courtesy of Chris Kidwell.

At Canyon Point, postcard.
Courtesy of Chris Kidwell.

View of Canaan Valley.
Courtesy of Chris Kidwell.

Straight road in Canaan Valley
near Davis, postcard.
Courtesy of Chris Kidwell.

Davis, 1908, postcard.
Courtesy of Chris Kidwell.

Leaving Canaan Valley on Route
32 looking towards Allegheny
Plateau, 1936, postcard; going
toward Harman.
Courtesy of Chris Kidwell.

Kelly Dicken
Family. *Left to
right:* Ilda, Bes-
sie Lee Bennett
Dicken (1876-
1966), Ruth
Lillian, Kelly
Dicken (1876-
1918), John, and
Olney. Kelly
was a foreman
at the Tannery,
Davis.
*Courtesy of
Chris Kidwell.*

Kelly and Bessie Dicken
home in Davis, postcard.
Courtesy of Chris Kidwell.

Greetings from Davis, postcard.
Courtesy of Chris Kidwell.

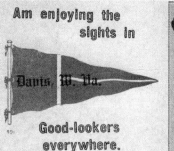

Am enjoying
the Sights in
Davis, post-
card.
*Courtesy of Chris
Kidwell.*

Robert Ward Eastham,
the first settler

Tucker County
Fair Program -- 1960.
Courtesy of Chris Kidwell.

Davis was incorporated in December 1889 and named for Henry Gassaway Davis, the owner and builder of the West Virginia Central & Pittsburgh Railway now the Western Maryland. It is 8,102 feet in altitude, the highest town in West Virginia, and its 1960 population was 804. The first settler in Davis was Robert Ward Eastham (1812-1924) who came from Rappahannock County, VA, and occupied a hunting camp in 1882. He was a swashbuckling, flamboyant Civil War guerilla, committed a murder in Parsons in 1897, escaped from jail and was never recaptured.

William Avenue,
Davis, July 4, 1910.
Courtesy of Ernest Arhar.
Submitted by Veronica Tekavec Staron.

"Red Men" gathering at the ball park, postcard.
Courtesy of Chris Kidwell.

Davis, circa 1915.
Courtesy of Ernest Arhar.
Submitted by Veronica Tekavec Staron.

Fireman of Davis, July 4, 1910.
Courtesy of Chris Kidwell.

Red Men, Davis, July 4, 1910, postcard.
Courtesy of Chris Kidwell.

Thomas Avenue, Davis, July 4, 1910, postcard.
Courtesy of Chris Kidwell.

Portions of Davis, postcard.
Courtesy of Chris Kidwell.

Davis, photo circa 1890s-1900s.
Photo by E.C. Miller, Davis.
Courtesy of Chris Kidwell.

Davis, photo.
Photo by Holyfield, Davis.
Courtesy of Chris Kidwell.

Davis, snow scene.
Courtesy of Chris Kidwell.

Bird's Eye View of Davis,
1911, postcard.
Courtesy of Chris Kidwell.

Photo of three-piece trio (guitar, clarinet and flute), circa 1900. The man in the middle is a conductor on the WV Central and Pittsburgh Railroad (notice his cap, watchchain and railroad lantern). Photo by Nestor Photo Company, Davis.
Courtesy of Chris Kidwell.

John Auvil (1885-1918), son of the Rev. John P. and Amelia Harsh Auvil. He was employed by the Pulp Mill in Davis when he left in November 1917, for a few days in Piedmont. His body was found by a young boy walking along the banks of the Potomac River in Cumberland, February 28, 1918. It was frozen in a cake of ice. His death remains a mystery.
Courtesy of Chris Kidwell.

A part of William Avenue, Davis, 1919, postcard.
Courtesy of Chris Kidwell.

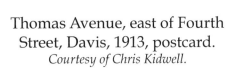

Thomas Avenue, east of Fourth Street, Davis, 1913, postcard.
Courtesy of Chris Kidwell.

Snow scene near Davis, postcard.
Courtesy of Chris Kidwell.

Snow scene on Seventh Street,
February 3, 1908, Davis, postcard.
Courtesy of Chris Kidwell.

Making apple cider lower end of Davis, postcard.
Courtesy of Chris Kidwell.

The Davis (Stumpfs) Orchestra circa 1905.
Theodore Stumpfs, Herbert Laker (violin),
James Marks, Fred N. Morins, Dr. Noah Wilson,
Mr. Jenkins and Myrtle Marks (violin).
Courtesy of Chris Kidwell from Keith Simmons.

Home of Alphonse and Carrie
Saunir, Davis, 1911, postcard.
Courtesy of Chris Kidwell.

Fourth Street, Davis, 1913, postcard.
Courtesy of Chris Kidwell.

Early wagon with children near Catholic Church on Kent Avenue, Davis, early 1890s.
Courtesy of Chris Kidwell.

Davis.
Courtesy of Chris Kidwell.

James William Kidwell (1871-1938) and son, Wade, photo dated 1915. Working on the Babcock Cattle Ranch fence for 12,000 acres, called the Marshall Track.
Courtesy of Chris Kidwell.

Sixth Street, Davis, 1911, postcard, (house on the left is John W. Wheeler's home, 1858-1928).
Courtesy of Chris Kidwell.

Thomas Avenue and Fifth Street, Davis, 1912, postcard. (Martha Caroline Reid Erhard (1848-1931), Ladies Furnishings Dry Goods Store).
Courtesy of Chris Kidwell.

West Virginia "boardinghouse" corner of William Avenue and Eighth Street. Owners, Thomas E. and Martha A. King, 1908, postcard.
Courtesy of Chris Kidwell.

Residence of Fred Viering,
Davis, 1909, postcard.
Courtesy of Chris Kidwell.

Kent Avenue,
Davis, postcard.
Courtesy of Chris Kidwell.

Fourth Street, Davis, 1915, postcard.
Courtesy of Chris Kidwell.

Thomas Avenue, Davis, postcard.
Courtesy of Chris Kidwell.

Going out to Davis toting guns to have some fun, postcard.
Courtesy of Chris Kidwell.

Fairfax Avenue, looking east, Davis, postcard.
Courtesy of Chris Kidwell.

National Bank of Davis, at the left, Davis, 1930s postcard.
Courtesy of Chris Kidwell.

Mountain City Band, organized in 1905, and incorporated in 1906, was widely known. This was a thirty-two-piece band and gave concerts, played in parades, at political meetings, for celebrations on many occasions, in the hometown and other towns; played in Elkins, in 1908, at the laying of the cornerstone of the West Virginia I.O.O.F. Home. In 1905, the band sponsored a three-day festival in the People's Opera House; proceeds used to buy uniforms. The main menu was buttered buns and small brook trout which were in great abundance in Blackwater River and tributaries. The only refrigeration was the icebox, so the members and friends of the Mountain City Band went to the river daily, catching the trout for the three-day event. Proceeds amounted to three hundred dollars, a good sum in 1905. Band uniforms were of a beautiful gray woolen material trimmed with black braid. Members were: Director, Herbert L. Blaker, Clarence Arbogast, Adam Stein, J.W. Kogelshatz, E.C. Widemire, Frederick N. Morin, L.H. Mott, John Johnston, Ray Dawson, Frank Heiskell, John Fauschenberger, Sherman Iden, Harry Weaver, Dr. N. McK. Wilson, Theodore Stumpf, Charles G. Stateer, Illaria Laconna, Harry Buckley, Robert C. McKelvey, Neil C. Heiskell, Charles Amlaw, Benson Unger, and Edwin Morin.
Courtesy of Chris Kidwell.

Mountain City Band in Parsons, July 3, 1909, postcard.
Courtesy of Chris Kidwell.

Canyon Point, Blackwater Canyon, Davis, postcard.
Courtesy of Jane H. Barb.

Davis, Pulp Mill Bridge.
Courtesy of Elmer "Slim" Moreland.
Submitted by Chris Kidwell.

Davis.
Courtesy of Elmer "Slim" Moreland.
Submitted by Chris Kidwell.

Davis area, Blackwater Falls Road, Boys' Camp, postcard.
Courtesy of Chris Kidwell.

"The season's catch of fur in Tucker, County, WV," postcard. Taken at Canaan Valley on the Carwell Place, *left to right*: Russell and Albert Knotts.
Courtesy of Chris Kidwell.

Union Tanning Company,
Davis, postcard.
Courtesy of Chris Kidwell.

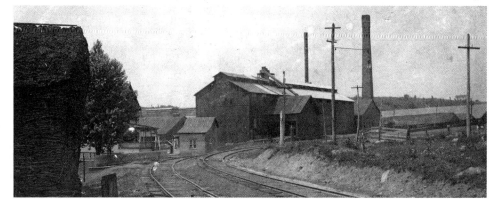

Union Tanning Company, Davis, 1907, postcard.
Courtesy of Chris Kidwell.

U.S. Leather Co., Davis West Va. Got Deed for Land May 1893

U.S. Leather Co.,
Davis, postcards.
Courtesy of Chris Kidwell.

Davis AERIE No. 936
F.O.E., Davis.
Courtesy of Chris Kidwell.

Davis,
photo by Holyfield.
Courtesy of Chris Kidwell.

Coal Tipple, Davis, 1895.
Courtesy of Chris Kidwell.

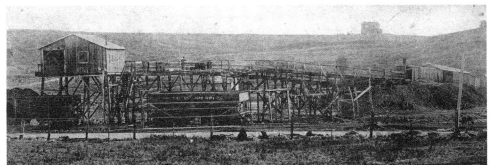

Blackwater Coal Co. Tipple, Davis, 1923, postcard.
Courtesy of Chris Kidwell.

Pulp Mill, Davis, postcard.
Courtesy of Chris Kidwell.

Davis Pulp Shed, Davis, 1896.
Courtesy of Chris Kidwell.

Pulp Mill, Davis, 1912, postcard.
Courtesy of Chris Kidwell.

28" trout, May 5, 1935, Blackwater River, Canaan Valley, near Davis. (It had a six inch Pike in it and took 45 minutes to land.)
Courtesy of Jane H. Barb.

Pulp Mill, Davis.
Courtesy of Ernest Arhar.
Submitted by Veronica Tekavec Staron.

Lumberyard, Davis.
Courtesy of Ernest Arhar. Submitted by Veronica Tekavec Staron.

Thompson Lumber Company, Davis.
Courtesy of Ernest Arhar. Submitted by Veronica Tekavec Staron.

Camps in Babcock Woods.
*Courtesy of Frances Tekavec.
Submitted by
Veronica Tekavec Staron.*

PICTURE PUZZLE: FIND TWO HEADS
The maiden and the old witch

MT. VIEW MOTEL
All rooms are efficiencies
Canaan Valley   Phone 304/866-4166
Route 32, 7 miles south of Davis
Mr. and Mrs. Guy R. Smith, Owners

Alford's Footlog, Beaver Creek, near Davis, postcard.
Courtesy of Chris Kidwell.

Mt. View Motel,
Davis, postcard.
Courtesy of Jane H. Barb.

Babcock's Box Factory, Davis, postcard.
Courtesy of Chris Kidwell.

Babcock Lumber Company, Davis, 1909, postcard.
Courtesy of Chris Kidwell.

Babcock Lumber Company,
Davis, postcard.
Courtesy of Chris Kidwell.

Babcock Job,
Davis, 1910, postcard.
Courtesy of Chris Kidwell.

Cutting crew on a Babcock
Lumber job, Davis, 1910,
postcard.
Courtesy of Chris Kidwell.

Going to work in Babcock
Woods, Davis, postcard.
Courtesy of Chris Kidwell.

Camps in Babcock Woods,
Davis, postcard.
Courtesy of Chris Kidwell.

A part of Babcock Lumber
and Boom Company, Davis.
Courtesy of Chris Kidwell.

Log engine wreck --
Babcock Lumber Company, Davis.
Courtesy of Chris Kidwell.

Wrecked bridge, Babcock Lumber and Boom Company, Davis,
1909, postcard.
Courtesy of Chris Kidwell.

Davis, postcard.
Courtesy of Chris Kidwell.

Fifty-foot long log, Davis,
postcard.
Courtesy of Chris Kidwell.

Pond at Mill #1, Davis, circa 1898.
Courtesy of Chris Kidwell.

A Mr. Dunwoody at Davis, 1890. Logs cut on
Col. Wm. H. Harness' land on west side of
Cooper Knob.
Courtesy of Chris Kidwell.

Log/train, Davis, postcard.
Courtesy of Chris Kidwell.

Babcock workers,
Davis, postcard.
Courtesy of Chris Kidwell.

An electrified train for lumbering or mining, Davis, postcard.
Courtesy of Chris Kidwell.

712 Western Maryland Railroad engine;
a Mr. Ruckel *in front*, postcard.
Courtesy of Chris Kidwell.

Snowbound engine, from February 1 to 4, 1908 between Thomas and Davis, 1911, postcard.
Courtesy of Chris Kidwell.

Railroad Station, Davis, 1911, postcard.
Courtesy of Chris Kidwell.

M. Depot, No. 2, Davis, 1909, postcard.
Courtesy of Chris Kidwell.

Davis Railroad station, postcard.
Courtesy of Chris Kidwell.

The "Black Handers" were at Davis, in the 1890s and 1900s. Billy Kidwell was attacked by one of the members but won the fight, taking a bone-handle knife from him. Kidwell received a sliced ear. This photo was taken at Fairmont.
Courtesy of Chris Kidwell.

The Black Handers weapons.
Courtesy of Chris Kidwell.

Babcock Lumber Company, Davis.
Courtesy of Chris Kidwell.

1954 GMC Wrecker owned by Meyer Motor Sales, Inc.,
1954-1973, Davis.
Courtesy of Susan Meyer.

Davis Drugstore operated by
John Sayger.
Courtesy of Ernest Arhar.
Submitted by Veronica Tekavec Staron.

Blackwater Lodge,
Davis, 1950s postcard.
Courtesy of Chris Kidwell.

Kindling Wood Factory,
Davis, 1915, postcard.
Courtesy of Chris Kidwell.

Envelope -- Beaver Creek
Lumber Company, Davis.
Courtesy of Chris Kidwell.

Key Tag for "Ros-
coe McDonald"
Davis Supply,
Co.
*Courtesy of
Chris Kidwell.*

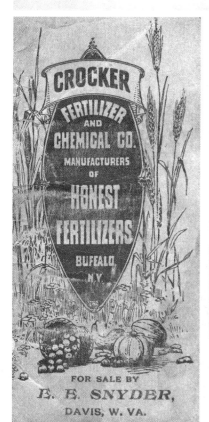

Crocker ad, 1896.
Courtesy of Chris Kidwell.

Stone Motel near Blackwater Falls, postcard, 1966.
Courtesy of Chris Kidwell.

Blackwater Hotel,
Davis, 1934, postcard.
Courtesy of Chris Kidwell.

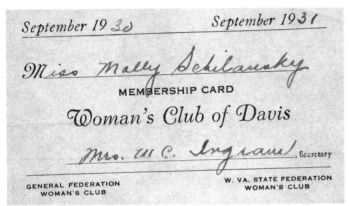

Peewee Golf Course, Davis,
1920s-1930s, postcard
Courtesy of Chris Kidwell.

Blackwater Hotel,
Davis, 1907, postcard.
Courtesy of Chris Kidwell.

Cooper's Restaurant, post-
card. Photo taken by Stan
Lambert, Parsons.
Courtesy of Chris Kidwell.

Timber crew, Davis, lunchtime in the woods.
Courtesy of Chris Kidwell.

Timber crew, Davis camp. *Man standing on far left* is Charlie Bodkin; *second row, second man seated,* Foster or John Guthrie; *back row, ninth man, left to right:* a Rev. Mr. Peters; thirteenth man, James Woods.
Courtesy of Chris Kidwell.

Timber crew, Davis. *Seventh man seated in the front row:* Frank Ray;
second man standing in back row: James Woods.
Courtesy of Chris Kidwell.

One of Guy Stringer's Railroad Logging crews, rails on logs, Babcock's Camp, Davis.
Ninth man in back row standing: Floyd Wright.
Courtesy of Chris Kidwell.

Worden's Hotel Restaurant, "Serving Good Food Since 1899," Davis, postcard.
Courtesy of Chris Kidwell.

Worden's Hotel, Davis.
Courtesy of Susan Meyer.

Hotel Howard, Davis.
Courtesy of Chris Kidwell.

Davis, postcard.
Courtesy of Chris Kidwell.

Anthony Degler & Sons, Davis -- Anthony and Catherine Deglar, natives of Germany, moved to Davis in 1889, operated a jewelry store and restaurant.
Courtesy of Chris Kidwell.

Harry W. Heironimus (1869-1912) at the H.W. Herionimus Clothier, Davis.
Courtesy of Chris Kidwell.

Erhard Bros. Jewelry Store,
Davis, postcard.
Courtesy of Chris Kidwell.

W.E. Weimer's Garage,
Davis.
Courtesy of Chris Kidwell.

MT. CITY GARAGE

W. E. WEIMER, Proprietor

Buick Authorized Sales and Service

G. M. C. TRUCKS

1928.
Courtesy of Chris Kidwell.

Verzi Saloon, Davis,
1900.
Courtesy of Ernest Arhar.
Submitted by
Veronica Tekavec Staron.

The Nestor Photo. Co.   Davis, W. Va.

Delton S. Jenkins and J.T. Darkey,
merchants, General Store in Davis.
Courtesy of Chris Kidwell.

Sam and Louisa Nestor Harsh who lived
on East Henry Avenue; built their own
home and blacksmith shop. Sam was
a blacksmith and Civil War veteran,
1836-1912; Louise, 1839-1922. Both are
buried in Davis Cemetery. Grandparents
of Wade Kidwell; moved to Davis circa
1890.
Courtesy of Chris Kidwell.

J.C. Burley Shop.
Courtesy of Frances Tekavec. Submitted by Veronica Tekavec Staron.

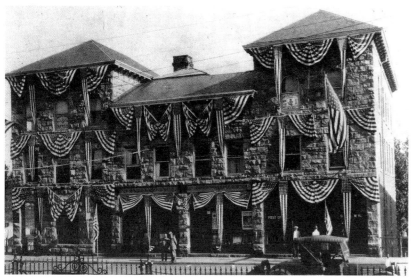

National Bank of Davis first homecoming, 1928, postcard.
Courtesy of Ernest Arhar.

National Bank Building,
Davis.
Courtesy of Frances Tekavec.
Submitted by
Veronica Tekavec Staron.

National Bank Building, Davis Depot and a part of the
Thompson Lumber Company, Davis.
Courtesy of Chris Kidwell.

Allegheny Heights and Sanitarium, Davis, 1909, postcard.
Courtesy of Chris Kidwell.

Allegheny Heights Hospital and Sanitarium, Davis, W. Va.

Allegheny Heights Hospital and Sanitarium, elevation 3,300 feet, Davis, postcard.
Courtesy of Ernest Arhar.

Brothers Jim and Wade Kidwell, circa 1928, with a whole deer mount done by Wade, East Henry Avenue, Davis.
Courtesy of Chris Kidwell.

Wade Kidwell shoveling snow in Davis, at Worden's Hotel where he worked, 1925.
Courtesy of Chris Kidwell.

Alice Harsh and William Kidwell, Davis.
Courtesy of Chris Kidwell.

Dan Means, Davis.
Courtesy of Chris Kidwell.

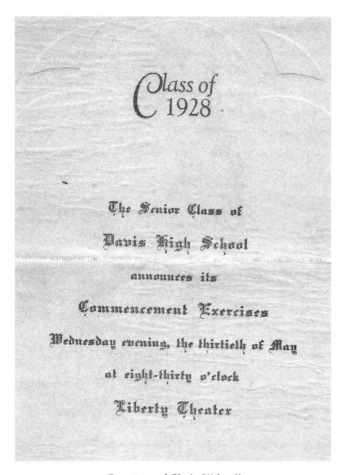

Courtesy of Chris Kidwell.

"Hockman" (Hutchinson style) soda bottle from Davis. Hugh B. Hockman in 1900 and 1901. According to RL Polk Business Directory, in 1900 and 1901, Hugh B. Hockman had a restaurant and confectionary store in Davis. There are only two known Hutchinson-type soda bottles with the name Hockman. The one in the photo came from an auction in Elkins.
Courtesy of Chris Kidwell.

Institute at Davis, while Harry S. Shaffer was Tucker County superintendent of schools.
Courtesy of Chris Kidwell.

Postcard of St. Veronica's Catholic Church, Davis, circa 1960s-1970s during the time that Father Charles Schneider served as pastor. St. Veronica's closed in 1992.
Courtesy of Susan Meyer.

A copy of an original painting of St. Veronica's Catholic Church owned by Josephine Gruden. The artist is unknown but the painting is now owned by Etta Golightly Martin. The painting is of the church prior to the 1906 lightning damage of the bell tower which was replaced.
Courtesy of Susan Meyer.

Catholic Church, Davis, postcard.
Courtesy of Ernest Arhar.

Presbyterian Church,
Davis, 1909, postcard.
Courtesy of Chris Kidwell.

1890s Free Methodist Church, Davis.
Courtesy of Chris Kidwell.

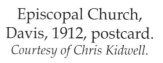

Methodist Episcopal Church,
South Davis, postcard.
Courtesy of Chris Kidwell.

Episcopal Church,
Davis, 1912, postcard.
Courtesy of Chris Kidwell.

Methodist Episcopal Church,
South Davis, postcard.
Courtesy of Chris Kidwell.

Lutheran Church, Davis, 1909, postcard.
Courtesy of Chris Kidwell.

Interior of St. John Lutheran Church,
Davis. Rev. A.F. Richardson, minister,
postcard.
Courtesy of Chris Kidwell.

Early Church in Davis, 1890s.
Courtesy of Chris Kidwell.

Davis, 1898. Samuel F. Harsh, *seated*, was a home guard at Philippi, during the Civil War. He owned a blacksmith shop. His wife, Louisa Nestor Harsh, *holding* Goldie Kidwell, moved to Davis around 1890. James William Kidwell, *standing*, worked for Babcock Lumber Company, as a boss. He also worked for Blackwater Coal Company. *Standing* with him is Sarah Alice Harsh Kidwell.
Courtesy of Chris Kidwell.

Frances Earl Lewis, circa 1900, born December 1894, son of J.H., a painter and boardinghouse proprietor, and Cornelius G. Lewis, Eighth Street, Davis.
Courtesy of Chris Kidwell.

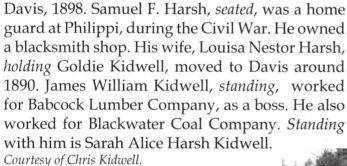

Harry Bergstrom at Kidwell hunting camp, 1920s.
Courtesy of Chris Kidwell.

Wade Kidwell at hunting camp near Davis on US 93.
Courtesy of Chris Kidwell.

Homeplace of Wade Kidwell, originally the home of Samuel and Louisa Harsh, East Henry Avenue. Later the home of William and Alice Harsh Kidwell.
Courtesy of Chris Kidwell.

Herman August Meyer 1856-1919.
Courtesy of Susan Meyer.

Mary Jackson Powell Meyer.
Courtesy of Susan Meyer.

Herman A. Meyer came to Davis in 1886 to serve as a teacher in the first school in Davis (1886-1889). He purchased the house now known as the Meyer House on Thomas Avenue from Mr. Thomas Burger July 19, 1898. The Meyer House was added to the National Register of Historical Places in 2010. In 1898, he started Meyer Insurance Agency which was one of the oldest insurance agencies in the state at the time of its sale in 1988. He was a director of the National Bank of Davis as well as president. He also served as a director at Miners and Merchants Bank. Mr. and Mrs. Meyer were active founding members of the Davis Presbyterian Church.

Herman Meyer.
Courtesy of Susan Meyer.

Blackwater Lodge, postcard.
Courtesy of Jane H. Barb.

Herman A. "Jim" Meyer, son of Edgar Meyer, owned and operated Meyer Motor Sales. Upon his father's death in 1953, he became owner of Meyer Insurance Agency. He served as mayor of Davis from 1947-1953 and 1967-1969.

Edgar G. "Waxie" Meyer, son of Herman Meyer, served as an agent for Meyer Insurance Agency after his father's death in 1919, as well as being an owner and operator of a garage and taxi service with W.E. Weimer. He was also part owner of the Meyer Transit Company. He was a director of the National Bank of Davis, vice president and president from 1942-1953.
Courtesy of Susan Meyer.

Christine Korosec Meyer, wife of Paul A. Meyer, was a school/county nurse for many years in Tucker County. She worked at the clinic in Davis that was operated by Dr. Samuel Bucher of Harman and was a nurse for the West Virginia Correctional Facility in Davis.

Paul Alphonsus Meyer, b. 1921.
Courtesy of Susan Meyer.

Christine Korosec Meyer, 1921-1987.
Courtesy of Susan Meyer.

Logging camp between Davis and Dobbin.
Courtesy of Chris Kidwell.

Left to right: Sisters Patricia Tekavec Cooper,
Jeannette Tekavec Ware and Alice Tekavec, Davis.
Courtesy of Veronica Tekavec Staron.

Hunters in Davis.
Courtesy of Veronica Tekavec Staron.

Three cub bears captured in Blackwater Canyon in 1911, by George Thompson, Squire Babcock and Fred Viering, postcard.
Courtesy of Jane H. Barb.

Deer Hunters, Davis.
Courtesy of Frances Tekavec.
Submitted by Veronica Tekavec Staron.

Butchering in Davis.
Courtesy of Veronica Tekavec Staron.

Lumbering in the 1920s, Davis.
Courtesy of Frances Tekavec. Submitted by Veronica Tekavec Staron.

Davis Fire Hall being built, 1890s.
Courtesy of Elmer "Slim" Moreland.
Submitted by Chris Kidwell.

Fireman's Hall, Davis, 1890s, postcard.
Courtesy of Chris Kidwell.

Davis Volunteer Fire Department.
Courtesy of Chris Kidwell.

Davis Fire Hall, 1890s.
Courtesy of Elmer "Slim" Moreland.
Submitted by Chris Kidwell.

Building a hunting cabin,
Davis, postcard.
Courtesy of Chris Kidwell.

Lodge #106, Davis, (*bottom left corner*, a Mr. Bogdonovich).
Courtesy of Frances Tekavec. Submitted by Veronica Tekavec Staron.

Davis lodge ribbon.
Courtesy of Chris Kidwell.

Davis.
Courtesy of Frances Tekavec. Submitted by Veronica Tekavec Staron.

Davis High School basketball team, 1922. *Right to left:* James Miller, Lynn Lantz, Holmes Arnold, Meriam Deale, Russell Helmick, Fredrick Meyers, Alford Dumas, Arnold Osbern, _____, _____, Coach Herbert Bosley.
Courtesy of Jane H. Barb.

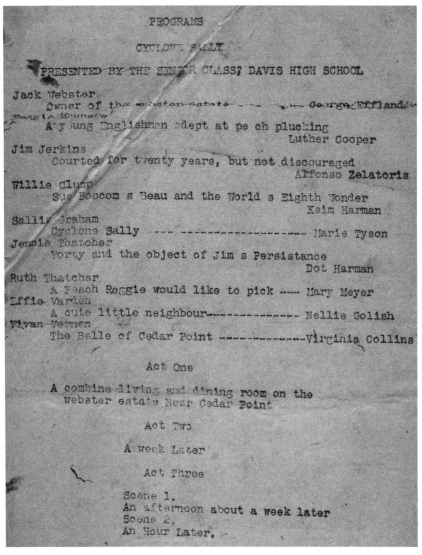

PROGRAMS

CYCLONE SALLY

PRESENTED BY THE SENIOR CLASS, DAVIS HIGH SCHOOL

Jack Webster
    Owner of the webster estate ------ George Effland
Reggie Monroe
    A young Englishman adept at peach plucking
                                                Luther Cooper
Jim Jerkins
    Courted for twenty years, but not discouraged
                                            Alfonso Zelatoris
Willie Clump
    Sue Boscom s Beau and the World s Eighth Wonder
                                                Keim Harman
Sallie Graham
    Cyclone Sally ----------------------- Marie Tyson
Jennie Thatcher
    Forty and the object of Jim s Persistance
                                                Dot Harman
Ruth Thatcher
    A Peach Reggie would like to pick ----- Mary Meyer
Effie Varden
    A cute little neighbour--------------- Nellie Golish
Vivan Vernon
    The Belle of Cedar Point -----------Virginia Collins

                    Act One

A combined living and dining room on the
    webster estate Near Cedar Point

                    Act Two

                A week Later

                Act Three

            Scene 1.
            An afternoon about a week later
            Scene 2.
            An Hour Later.

Davis High School play, 1928.
Courtesy of Chris Kidwell.

Faculty of Davis High School in front of the school, 1955-1956. *Front row left to right*: a Miss Windell, Miss Anna Bogdonavich, Nelly Crossland; *back row*: Virginia Cooper, Mr. McDowell and Mildred Eschelman.
Courtesy of Alice Tekavec.

Davis High School Class of 1928.
Courtesy of Chris Kidwell.

PROGRAM

Invocation .... Rev. A. F. Richardson
Chorus .... Senior Class
Salutatory .... George Effland
Chorus .... Senior Class
Address — Dr. A. Pelzer Wagener, W. Va. University
Awarding of Diplomas, E. L. Gibson, Prin. H. School
Valedictory .... Nellie Golish
Chorus .... Senior Class

CLASS OFFICERS

PRESIDENT, Herman Lewis
VICE PRESIDENT, George Effland
SECY.-TREAS., Mary Jackson Meyer

CLASS ROLL

Russell Arnold	Alfonse Zelatoris
Luther Cooper	Virginia Collins
George Effland	Nellie Golish
Keim Harman	Dorothy Harman
Wade Kidwell	Marie Tyson
Herman Lewis	

CLASS SPONSOR

Mrs. H. M. Painter

Davis High School Commencement Program.
Courtesy of Chris Kidwell.

Davis High School
Commencement Program.
Courtesy of Chris Kidwell.

Davis High School.
Courtesy of Veronica Tekavec Staron.

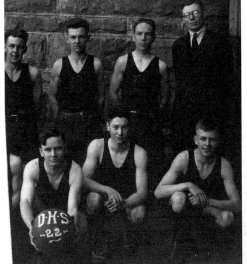

Davis High School Basketball
Team, 1922. *Left to right, top
row*: Holmes Arnold, Russell
Helmick, Lynn Lantz, Coach
_____; *bottom row*: James
Miller, Arnold Osbern, and
Fredrick Meyers.
Courtesy of Jane H. Barb.

Davis High School, 1910, postcard.
Courtesy of Chris Kidwell.

Davis High School All-Class Reunion -- Blackwater Falls.
Courtesy of Chris Kidwell.

Davis High School baseball team, The Mountaineers, 1916. *Front row, seated left to right*: E. Harman, Wise Mountain, Berl Lear, Wade Wilson. *Second row*: Philip Fox, Earl Spreadberry, Gilbert Riddle, Frank Wilhem, Herbert Bosley, Harry Snyder, Smith Hockman, and Rouse Colvin.
Courtesy of Chris Kidwell.

Davis basketball team. The first Davis basketball team members were Verne Hall, Ray (Slip) Slider, Gail Strader, Ova Burley, Bill Harman and Walter Riddle. Team was organized in 1910 or 1911.
Courtesy of Chris Kidwell.

Davis, baseball, 1914, postcard. Among the players were: Musty Suffers, pitcher; Aldine Poling, catcher; "Tuck" Eddy, third base; Ivan (Rugby) Poling, short-stop; Patsy Clark, first base; James Buckley, outfield; Red Wiles, Claude Campbell, _____ Miller, Harry Adams, Bill Hamilton and Malone Gaynor.
Courtesy of Chris Kidwell.

Ice skating around 1908, Davis, Blackwater River, post-card.
Courtesy of Chris Kidwell.

Davis High School football team, 1925.
Courtesy of Elmer "Slim" Moreland. Submitted by Chris Kidwell.

Davis High School Girls' basketball team, 1922. *Back row, right to left*: Dorothy Carrington, Carry Harper, Coach Kathy Clark, _____, Hallie Lawrence and Murnie Mountain.
Courtesy of Jane H. Barb.

Davis Cornet Band.
Courtesy of Jane H. Barb.

The Bava Family, family's home, Davis, postcard: John, Janet, Lucy and Juanita.
Courtesy of Jane H. Barb.

Dolly Sods wilderness
and scenic area.
Courtesy of Jane H. Barb.

Canaan Valley.
Courtesy of June H. Barb.

Bear Rocks, Dolly Sods.
Courtesy of Jane H. Barb.

Photo taken on S.F. Harsh's farm in Canaan Valley. Standing by hay wagon with pitchfork, Samuel F. Harsh, 1836-1912. Louisa Harsh standing at very end of hay wagon.
Courtesy of Chris Kidwell.

Winter at Davis, 1923, postcard.
Courtesy of Ernest Arhar.

Blackwater Falls, Davis.
Courtesy of Chris Kidwell.

Blackwater Lodge, postcard.
Courtesy of Ray and Lucille Adams.

Unknown fishermen on Blackwater River.
Courtesy of Chris Kidwell.

The first funeral director in Davis was Lucien Howe Mott (Mar. 2, 1974 - Mar. 16, 1974), beginning in 1901. His sign read, "L.H. Mott, Undertaker and Cabinetmaker." Lucien was married to Pearl Digman Mott (Feb. 13, 1885 - Apr. 25, 1978). The funeral home remains where it was originally established, 567 Thomas Avenue, Davis.

Photos courtesy of Hinkle Funeral Home.

Pap and Granny's wedding photos.

In the 1940s, Wayne C. Spiggle purchased the funeral home and sold it to Lester R. "Bucky" Hinkle, a Silver Star veteran from World War II, and Barbara McDowell. "Bucky" Hinkle retired in 1977 but remained active until his death, Nov. 10, 2009. Lester and Barbara's son, G. Scott Hinkle is the funeral director (2011) and worked alongside his wife, Diane White Hinkle from 1987-1997.

Funeral homes provided ambulance service to the community until the 1980s when emergency squads became active in West Virginia. Lester and Scott Hinkle provided the first Emergency Medical Squad classes to Tucker County residents.

Robert T. (III) and Anita Love Barton gave Canaan Valley its "...first commercial skiing facility south of the Mason-Dixon Line....(*Cumberland Sunday Times*, 1959). They are credited with having brought tourism to its Zenith in Tucker County. The Bartons owned Weiss Ski Shop and are pictured here at the 1965 Alpine Festival.
Courtesy of Annie Snyder.

The Ben F. Thompson family with painting in background of the original family farmhouse named "Willows," built by his parents, George and Elise Thompson in 1914 in Canaan Valley. Behind Mr. Thompson is their daughter, Sarah M. Thompson Fletcher, his wife, Barbra Dorothy Mayor Thompson, and their son, Frank Howard Thompson. Mr. Thompson managed a banana plantation in Guatemala and a sugar cane plantation in Cuba before returning to a life in Canaan Valley. Dorothy received a National Folk Heritage fellowship from the National Endowment of the Arts for her weaving skills and teaching of the art.
Courtesy of Mariwyn McClain Smith.

Horse-drawn carriage took early skiers to Weiss Knob ski area in Canaan Valley, on the Randall Reed Farm. It is now the White Grass Cross Country, on Freeland Road, run by Chip Chase and his wife, Laurie Little.
Courtesy of Mariwyn McClain Smith.

Skiing on Cabin Mountain near Davis

1950s, postcard.

1966, postcard.

Skiing at Cabin Mountain and Weiss Knob,
ten miles from Worden's Hotel, Davis, postcard.
Courtesy of Chris Kidwell.

Other Areas in Tucker County . . .

Arch and Phoebe Bright Carr family home on Mill Run,
Mozart Mountain near Gladwin, Dry Fork River Valley.
Courtesy of Flossie Hardy.

William Mack Bright and
Thomas W. Bright, Gladwin.
Courtesy of Flossie Hardy.

Abel Norman "Son" Long (June 27, 1877-Aug. 24, 1952) and wife, Boena Teter Long (Aug. 19, 1874-Feb. 9, 1947) with baby. "Son" was a well-known bear hunter of the Dry Fork River Valley.
Courtesy of Flossie Hardy.

Mary Frances Cooper, sister to Martha Alice
Cooper Bright, Gladwin, Mozart Mountain, Dry
Fork River Valley.
Courtesy of Flossie Hardy.

William Lee and Solome Cooper Wymer,
Gladwin.
Courtesy of Flossie Hardy.

Marion Carr, Emma Carr
Bonner's father, Mozart
Mountain, Dry Fork River
Valley.
Courtesy of Flossie Hardy.

Standing, Ben and Delphia B. Johnson;
seated George Johnson and Orpha
Bright Murphy, Gladwin.
Courtesy of Flossie Hardy.

Indiana Long, Otter Creek. Lived
to be over 100 years old; Gladwin.
Courtesy of Flossie Hardy.

Left to right: Thomas W. Bright and Harvey Murphy logging on Mozart Mountain.
Courtesy of Flossie Hardy.

Logging on Mozart Mountain (Green Mountain) on the Dry Fork River near Hendricks. *Front left to right*: Thomas W. Bright, *in back standing on log*; John Add Bright, *holding two horses*, Jerry Harper, *holding two horses*; *back row*: unknown and George Kenny Bright, holding crosscut saw.
Courtesy of Flossie Hardy.

This house was built for Thom W. and Martha A. Bright circa 1900 on Mozart Mountain facing Mill Run (now US Rt. 72) on Dry Fork River. *Left to right on porch*: Thomas Wesley Bright, Adman Harper (*seated*), William McKinley Bright, Martha Alice Cooper Bright, John Add Bright, Mary Ann Teter Bright, Orpha Ann Bright Murphy, Bessie Bright Harper, Annie Bonner Bright holding Pearl Marie Bright, George Kenny Bright (husband of Annie Bright), Clarence Bright, Lenzy Bright and Emmett Bright, close Gladwin.
Courtesy of Flossie Hardy.

Left to right: John Add, Thomas W., Delphia F., Martha Alice Cooper and (*in front*) Orpha Mae Bright, Mozart Mountain near Gladwin.
Courtesy of Flossie Hardy.

Harvey and Orpha Bright Murphy, May 21, 1916, Gladwin.
Courtesy of Flossie Hardy.

Ed and Lizzie Bright Long's
home and tree nursery, Gladwin.
Courtesy of Flossie Hardy.

Ben and Delphia Bright Johnson with
children George (*standing*) and baby
Vivian; Gladwin.
Courtesy of Flossie Hardy.

Mary Teter Bright, Flossie Bright Hardy's mother's
homeplace, destroyed in 1985 flood. Dry Fork, Gladwin.
Courtesy of Flossie Hardy.

Fourth from the left: Benjamin Franklin
White, son of Laban White, Jenningston,
postcard.
Courtesy of Chris Kidwell.

Jenningston

Left to right: Grover Carr, _____, Jonas Carr, Grover
Smith, John Spitzer, and _____, Jenningston, postcard.
Courtesy of Chris Kidwell.

Left to right: _____, Jonas Carr, James Woods, _____, Bean Carr, _____, Jenningston, postcard.
Courtesy of Chris Kidwell.

Miller Hill

Miller Hill, July 1952, looking toward Parsons.
Courtesy of Ray and Lucille Adams.

D.F. Railroad crew, Jenningston.
Courtesy of Chris Kidwell.

Front row: Elmo, Robin and Ruth Miller (?). *Middle row*: George, Camden and Nora Miller. *Back row*: Kenneth, Ethel, _____, and Elsie Miller.
Courtesy of Ray and Lucille Adams.

Miller Place.
Courtesy of Ray and Lucille Adams

Camden and Nora Adams Miller family.
Back row: Camden, Nora, Ethel, Selby Adams and Elsie.
Courtesy of Ray and Lucille Adams.

Group of men exploring Big Springs Cave, on McGowan Mountain commonly, called Twin Springs because one spring drains into Otter Creek and another into Elk Lick Run -- close to Hendricks/Hambleton. *Third man from the left* is a Griffith.
Courtesy of Chris Kidwell.

Bill Carr -- first automobile fatality in Tucker County.
Courtesy of Chris Kidwell.

Auviltown School -- Jay Moran, teacher.
Courtesy of Chris Kidwell.

Auviltown

Elizabeth and Joshua Robinson at the Robinson Hill store that they owned from 1899-1905, in Hannahsville on the old county road (also known as Louse Camp Run).
Courtesy of their great-grandon, Jim Root.

Auviltown.
Courtesy of James and Robert Auvil.

George and Anna Bishoff with Mable Auvil and some Bishoff cousins.
Courtesy of James and Robert Auvil.

Jimmie Dale and Donnie Keith Auvil.
Courtesy of James and Robert Auvil.

Gay Auvil -- one year old.
Courtesy of James and Robert Auvil.

George Auvil (occupation, farmer) and family.
Courtesy of James and Robert Auvil.

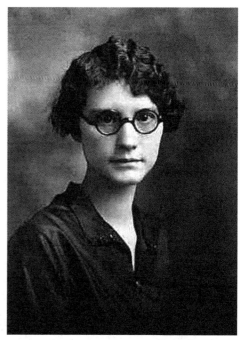

Mable Auvil.
Courtesy of James and Robert Auvil.

J.L. Auvil Store.
Courtesy of James and Robert Auvil.

George Bishoff Family. George F. Bishoff, 23, married Ann Eliza Auvil, 22, June 12, 1879. He was the son of John Bishoff and she was the daughter of John and Catherine Auvil.
Courtesy of James and Robert Auvil.

In 1845, John Auvil, a native of Pennsylvania, moved to Pifer Mountain, Tucker County with his wife Catherine, from Barbour County. He moved into Auviltown where he built a grist mill. He built a dam across Cheat River and operated the mill by water power. In 1890, a post office was established at Auviltown with George B. Auvil , a son of John Auvil, as post master.

Courtesy of James and Robert Auvil. Information from History of Tucker County by Homer Floyd Fansler. Published by McClain Printing Company.

Monnie Auvil, granddaughter of John and Catherine Auvil.
Courtesy of James and Robert Auvil.

Robinson Hill and Louse Camp Run

Hauling lumber near Auviltown, Bull Run.
Note the great old birdhouse, postcard.
Courtesy of Chris Kidwell.

Jacob Henry Robinson, (June 21, 1868 -.September 25, 1928), m. January 15, 1896, to Columbia Alice Miller, (January 12, 1871 - February 23, 1962), daughter of Daniel and Abigail Wilt Miller. Also pictured baby Lula Jane Robinson (Shahan), (December 11, 1896 - February 13, 1997). Jacob and Alice raised their family on Robinson Hill.
Courtesy of Jeannette Shahan.

Elizabeth Spangler, (May 2, 1841 - March 21, 1917), daughter of Jacob and Mary Weaver Spangler, married Joshua Robinson, May 22, 1834. Joshua Robinson, (February 15, 1834 - August 24, 1921), the son of John O. and Rebecca Day Robinson. Joshua was a farmer, blacksmith, and merchant, owning 109 acres on Louse Camp Run, also known as Robinson Hill Farm. They are buried on Robinson Hill. Joshua marked Elizabeth's grave with a hemlock tree.
Courtesy of Jeannette Shahan.

No. 5 Licking Creek School, 1965.
Courtesy of Jeannette Shahan.

Shahan twins, *left to right*:
Alton and Allen, b. August 10, 1925.
Courtesy of Jeannette Shahan.

Philip Shahan family-- *Front row left to right*: Gay Tona, (March 1, 1899 - January 5, 1974); Philip Nelson, (September 9, 1849 - January 22, 1913), Barbara Bowman Shahan, (August 18, 1864 - May 3, 1946), holding baby Bertha Nestor, (April 10, 1910 - December 9, 1967); and Waitman Philip, (September 26, 1904 - February 9, 1953). *Back row*: Alta Wilson, (July 21, 1896 - September 24, 1918); Datis Alvin, (November 11, 1887 - August 3, 1955); Ernest U., (October 14, 1885 - October 22, 1969) Florence Lulu Shahan, (June 20, 1893 - March 16, 1983), Elizabeth Ina Nestor, (May 29, 1890 - February 4, 1969).
Courtesy of Jeannette Shahan.

September 1954, *left to right*: Arthur, Arlie, Ben and George Myers at their homeplace at the head of Louse Camp Run.
Courtesy of Jeannette Shahan.

On the roof of the shed at the Robinson Hill school are *left to right*: Ira Shahan, Guy Robinson, Woodrow Robinson, Mae Myers, and Gay Shahan.
Courtesy of Jeannette Shahan.

Alice Miller Robinson and her children *left to right*: Bill Robinson, Flossie Nestor, Straudie Compton, Lessie Root, Millie Grandstaff, Russell Robinson, Lula Shahan, and Ernest Miller.
Courtesy of Jeannette Shahan.

Known as Grandma Barbara, Barbara Bowman Shahan, (August 18, 1864 - May 3, 1946), helped deliver many babies. She lived on Licking Creek and lived to see her twin grandsons Allen and Alton Shahan return from World War II.
Courtesy of Jeannette Shahan.

Arthur Moore School Group, Robinson Hill. Teacher Arthur Moore *on the far right* and Jacob Robinson *in the back at the tree*.
Courtesy of Jeannette Shahan.

Alice Miller Robinson.
Courtesy of Jeannette Shahan.

Shahan boys raised on a farm on Licking Creek. *Left to right:* Allen, Alton, Wilson, Virgil and Gerald.
Courtesy of Jeannette Shahan.

Mary C. Burns Myers Family, *left to right*: Ethel, Arthur, Lucretia, Mary C., Arlie, and (*in front*) Jessie. They lived at the head of Louse Camp Run.
Courtesy of Jeannette Shahan.

Left to right: Twins Alton G., (August 10, 1925 - November 16, 2008); and Allen R. Shahan, d. December 18, 1998, grew up on the Shahan place on Licking Creek and attended No. 5 School. They were drafted and served with the 69th Infantry in Europe during World War II. They were married by the Rev. Mr. O'Dell in Parsons on October 2, 1949, to sisters Beulah (Alton) and Beryl (Allen) Meyers.
Courtesy of Jeannette Shahan.

Home of John L. and Mary Catherine Burns Myers at the head of Louse Camp Run.
Courtesy of Jeannette Shahan.

Jacob Henry Robinson, (June 21, 1868 - September 25, 1928), m. January 15, 1896, to Columbia Alice Miller, (January 12, 1871 - February 23, 1962), daughter of Daniel and Abigail Wilt Miller.
Courtesy of Jeannette Shahan.

Front row left to right: Kenneth, Beryl and Beulah Myers; *back row left to right*: Chloe Robinson, Henrietta Hershman Myers and Arlie Myers. Head of Louse Camp Run.
Courtesy of Jeannette Shahan.

60th Wedding Anniversary, of Ernest and Lula Jane Robinson Shahan, October 1963. *In front:* Ernest and Lula Shahan; *middle row left to right*: Darl, Walt, Jerd, Virgil and Wilson; *back row*: Ira, Gay, Anetta Shahan Creekmore, Everett, Edith Shahan Koob, Alton and Allen.
Courtesy of Jeannette Shahan.

Arlie and Henrietta Hershman Myers Family. *Front row left to right*: Walter, Gay, Junior, Paul and Karl; *back row*: Arlie Myers, Henrietta Hershman Myers, Beulah, Beryl, Kenneth and Beatrice.
Courtesy of Jeannette Shahan.

Alice Miller and Jacob Henry Robinson with children *left to right:* Lessie, Straudie, Lula, Millie and Ernest Miller. They raised their family on the Robinson Hill. *Courtesy of Jeannette Shahan.*

Mary C. Burns Myers family, summer of 1900. *Boys left to right*: William, Benjamin, George, James; Ethel *on her mother's (Mary C.) lap*, Lucretia and Virginia. They lived at the head of Louse Camp Run. *Courtesy of Jeannette Shahan.*

Robinson Hill Gathering. *Front row left to right, sitting:* Arlie Myers, _____ Robinson, Lula Robinson and _____ Robison (the rest of the row unknown).

Eppilonia Goff,
(August 1, 1841 - April 5, 1930).
Courtesy of Jeannette Shahan.

John Wesley Chambers was a Methodist minister, (October 8, 1834 - d. June 26, 1908), m. February 18, 1858 to Eppilonia Goff. They lived on the Chambers Place at Seven Islands and are both buried there.
Courtesy of Jeannette Shahan.

Woods foreman and cook and cookees camp, 2 Red Creek, near Dry Fork, 1912, postcard.
Courtesy of Jane H. Barb.

Camp crew,
right-hand prong of Red Creek.
Courtesy of Jane H. Barb.

Early Rumbarger's Saw Mill after a fire, circa late 1880s-1890s, Dobbin.
Courtesy of Chris Kidwell.

Old Swinging Bridge at the Fraley Place along Dry Fork River on Dry Fork Railroad Grade. Flood of 1985 washed it away. This was the trail that led to Shaver's Mountain Community near Gladwin. The bridge was on the dirt road off US 72.
Courtesy of Chris Kidwell.

Pile Skidway,
Horseshoe Run, postcard.
Courtesy of Jane H. Barb.

Laneville

Log train at Laneville.
Photo from the Ed Simmons Family. Courtesy of Chris Kidwell.

Log loader at Laneville.
Photo from the Ed Simmons Family.
Courtesy of Chris Kidwell.

Boardinghouse, April 21, 1912, called Cooper House.
Run by John Cooper Family, Jenningston.
Courtesy of Chris Kidwell.

Dry Fork Railroad at Jenningston, 1924. The Jenningston Store is on the right; the Depot is on the left. Kids are standing on railroad ties; tracks had been removed.
Courtesy of Chris Kidwell.

Asa Harman, Jr.'s Restaurant and Store, Laneville, circa 1905-1910.
Courtesy of Chris Kidwell.

1890s Davis Coal and Coke Coketon Colliery, Douglas.
Courtesy of Chris Kidwell.

Stoney River
Dam in Tucker
County.
*Courtesy of
Chris Kidwell.*

Back row, second from left by tree is Frank Harr; *third* is Elwood Roy *(arms crossed holding ax); front row, seated* is _____, Red Creek postcard.

Red Creek
Flanagan Hill
Courtesy of Chris Kidwell.

Postcard includes Harrison Roy.

Unknown, postcard.

R.M. Hallett, postcard.

Woman on left: Melvina Flanagan Bonner, 1885-1937, daughter of Stuart Flanagan., postcard.

Left to right: Jake Roby and Ole Keister, postcard.

Flanagan Hill store and post office, Red Creek,
built in 1900 by Robert Raines and Dan Judy.
Courtesy of Chris Kidwell.

Red Creek Store and post office, postcard.
Courtesy of Chris Kidwell.

Mt. View

PUBLIC SCHOOL

DISTRICT No. 4.

RED CREEK P. O., TUCKER CO., W. VA.

C. I. SMITH, TEACHER.

Pupils.

Pompey Smith	W. L. Lambert
M. V. Bennett	French Smith
Willie J. Carr	Jerry H. Smith
S. C. Wilfong	Isom H. Carr
A. L. George	Cecil C. George
Ira F. Teter	J. W. Arbogast
Mc C. Flanagan	Sol. Flanagan
Lester Flanagan	Jasper Johnson
Luther G. George	
Margie C. Bennett	Floda V. Lambert
Elsie V. Lambert	Cora E. Bennett
Laura Pennington	Minnie E. Lambert
Florence B. Lambert	Rosa Lambert
Lela Lambert	D. May Flynn
Maude E. Flynn	Zeona Arbogast
Jennie Smith	Floda Johnson
Bessie L. Bennett	Lillie Carr
Gracie D. Bennett	

Trustees.

T. G. Montony,	A. C. Lambert,
A. B. Carr.	

1903, Mt. View Public School.
Courtesy of Chris Kidwell.

Red Creek Log Engine, postcard.
Courtesy of Chris Kidwell.

Logging on Speeder,
Red Creek.
Courtesy of Chris Kidwell.

Boyd Flanagan, b. January 1890, son of Stuart Flanagan, Red Creek, 1907.
Courtesy of Chris Kidwell.

Left to right: Herman Lambert,
Jeff Jasper Hedrick and French
Raines.
Courtesy of Chris Kidwell.

Left to right: Lindsey Reed, Jeff Hedrick,
Asa Bonner and French Raines.
Laneville/Red Creek, postcard.
Courtesy of Chris Kidwell.

H.W. and Mary J. Flanagan Bonner,
his second wife, Red Creek.
Courtesy of Chris Kidwell.

Laneville/Red Creek,
front row seated on left,
Joseph Hickman.
Courtesy of Chris Kidwell.

Flanagan Hill/Red Creek School (a one-room school near the store/post office).
Courtesy of Chris Kidwell.

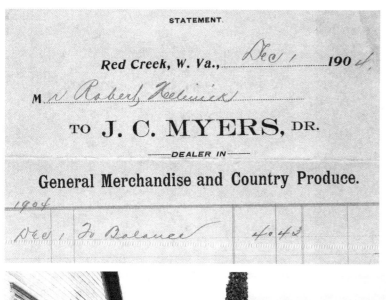

STATEMENT.

Red Creek, W. Va., _Dec 1_ 190_4_

M__ _Robert Helmick_

TO **J. C. MYERS**, DR.

—DEALER IN—

General Merchandise and Country Produce.

1904

Dec 1 | To Balance | | 40 43

Bluff near
Red Creek Junction, postcard.
Courtesy of Chris Kidwell.

Lambert Family Reunion, held at Flanagan Hill Church,
Red Creek, August 4, 1935.
Courtesy of Chris Kidwell.

Front row, left to right: Carrie
Smith, Ruth Lambert and Tina
Kisamore; *back row:* Glen Ault,
Shirley Cooper and Lincoln
Smith, Red Creek/Flanagan
Hill, postcard.
Courtesy of Chris Kidwell.

Little Jim Flanagan and
Grant Watts, Flanagan Hill.
Courtesy of Chris Kidwell.

Left to right: Carrie and Orpha
Smith, Red Creek/Flanagan
Hill, postcard.
Courtesy of Chris Kidwell.

Gordon and Rella Lambert with children Meredith and Harper, Christmas 1925, Red Creek, postcard.
Courtesy of Chris Kidwell.

Front row, left to right: Hard Smith, Edith Smith, Dora Bonner and Bertie Bonner Rennix; *back row:* Eva Bonner, Carrie Smith, Susan Smith and Verna Lambert Bonner, Red Creek, 1923, postcard.
Courtesy of Chris Kidwell.

Eva Gladys Bonner, b. Mar. 13, 1908; Bertie Alice Bonner, b. Sept. 4, 1915 and Dora Katherine Bonner, b. Sept. 8, 1919, Red Creek.
Courtesy of Chris Kidwell.

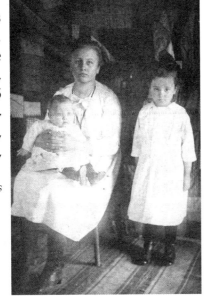

Jessie Hall Lambert *on right*, Red Creek.
Courtesy of Chris Kidwell.

Henry Smith, Red Creek, postcard.
Courtesy of Chris Kidwell.

Speeders at Jenningston circa 1908. *Left to right, standing*: Perry Hedrick, Jones Carr, James Woods, Date Carr, Adam Elza, Harry Vance, William White, Grover Carr (*holding dog*), Albert Elza and Lee Champ, _____, Hiner Waybright (*behind*), Isom Judy (*front*), Albert Carr, _____(boy); *sitting*: Lee Wimer, Ken Kerens, Robert Kerns, _____, Doyle Sturms, _____, _____ Brooks, and Kenny Mullennex.
Courtesy of Chris Kidwell.

Left to right, seated: Howard Raines and Cora Judy Harper; back row: Ora Raines and Annie C. Tingler Judy, (Oct. 16, 1865 - Nov. 15, 1905).

Shaver's Mountain
Courtesy of Chris Kidwell.

"Clel" McClellan Judy (1864-1931) and Jackson White, 1931.

Glen Judy Family. *Front row, left to right*: Junior, Glen, Martha, and Betty Lou; *middle row*: Glenda, Thelma and John; *back row*: Georgia, Bess, Maycelle, and Dorothy. Glen was the son of Clel and Annie Tingler Judy, Shaver's Mountain.

Shaver's Mountain School. *Front row, left to right*: Denzil Lee Judy, Carrie Showalter and Bill Judy; *back row*: Charlie Showalter, Denver Judy, Dessie Judy and Jack Judy.

Shaver's Mountain Farm. Sons of Isom and Gertie Judy, *left to right*: Dickson, Denver Harness, "Jack" Dennis, Denzil Lee, John William, and Howard Ray.
Courtesy of Chris Kidwell.

Sponaugle Family. *Front row, left to right*: Ab Larry, Bricy, Bessie, Tess, Clarence, Tiny, _____, and Lenny; *back row*: John, Isabelle, and Willie Bodie.
Courtesy of Chris Kidwell.

Shaver's Mountain, 1930s. Children of Isom and Gertie Judy, *left to right*: Denver, Dessie, Dennis "Jack," and Denzil "Lee" Judy. Taken on Ray Long's car.
Courtesy of Chris Kidwell.

Front row, left to right: Tiny Sponaugle, Osborn Bodkin and Jessie Sponaugle Bodkin; *back row*: Bessie (twin to Jessie), Alvin Sponaugle and Dessie Hedrick Sponaugle, Shaver's Mountain.
Courtesy of Chris Kidwell.

Ed and Lizzie Bright Long, Shaver's Mountain.
Courtesy of Chris Kidwell.

John Long, Shaver's Mountain.
Courtesy of Chris Kidwell.

Lizzie Bright (*seated on right*) and friend. Shaver's Mountain.
Courtesy of Chris Kidwell.

Oscar Bill Bodkin,
Shaver's Mountain, postcard.
Courtesy of Chris Kidwell.

Shaver's Mountain, postcard. *Front row, left to right*: Odis, Luther and Floyd Bodkin, Tiny Sponaugle, Osborn Bodkin, Dolly Mullennex, Isom Bodkin and Willey Cunningham; *back row*: John Bodkin (with Baby Keister), Lovie Cunningham Bodkin, Ben Bodkin, Charlie Mullennex, Alby Cunningham, Bill Bodkin, Winton Judy, Susan White, Elva Cunningham and Omer Bodkin.
Courtesy of Chris Kidwell.

House on Shaver's Mountain known as the "Sponaugle Place" and "Judy Place". Isom Judy and his sons built the home.
Courtesy of Chris Kidwell.

Jessie Sponaugle Bodkin.
Shaver's Mountain, postcard.
Courtesy of Chris Kidwell.

Shaver's Mountain School. *Front row, left to right*: Jack Judy, Charlie Showalter, Bill Judy, _____ Waybright and Denzil Judy; *back row*: Carrie Showalter, Ruth Kidwell, teacher, and _____ Waybright. *Courtesy of Chris Kidwell.*

Shaver's Mountain. *Left to right*: Susan Long Showalter, Lucinda (mother) Long, and Ella Moore Long (wife of H.C. Long). *Courtesy of Chris Kidwell.*

Fred "Bluehead" Mullennex, Shaver's Mountain. *Courtesy of Chris Kidwell.*

Shaver's Mountain, postcard. *Left to right*: Isom Judy and "Buzz" Truman Arbogast. *Courtesy of Chris Kidwell.*

Shaver's Mountain, postcard. *Left to right*: Osborn Bodkin and Clarence Hartmen. *Courtesy of Chris Kidwell.*

Gertrude Judy, wife of Isom Judy, riding a horse across Dry Fork River at Ridge Ford from their farm on Shaver's Mountain. *Courtesy of Chris Kidwell.*

R.L. Polk West Virginia Gazateer
1881 to 1964
Dunn and Bradstreet
Researched by Chris Kidwell
1882-1883 Towns with post offices:
Alum Hill, Holly Meadows, Leadmine, Pheasant Run, Red Creek and Texas.

The Mercantile Agency, July 1889

1. Alum Hill -- Philippi Banking Town
    L.D. Corrick & Co., grain dealer, flour mill
    Abraham Currance, mercantile mill
    Moss, general store
    J.W. Piter & Co.
    M. H. Scott, sawmill

2. Auvil -- Philippi Banking Town (population 20)
    Dr. T.M. Austin, general store
    John Auvil, grist and sawmill
    George Bishop, blacksmith
    M.S. Phillips & Sons, general store

3. Canaan -- Piedmont Banking Town (population 100)
    Canaan Boom and Lumber Co.

4. Courtlands -- Philippi Banking Town (population 10)
    Ell Nines General Store

5. Davis -- Piedmont Banking Town (population 600)
    Ash and Lashly, general store
    Bass Bros., clothing
    Blackwater Boom & Lumber Co.
    A. Deglar, jeweler
    Thomas Donahue, saloon
    R.W. Eastham, general store
    George Elbon, furniture
    W.H. Evans, sawmill
    Fayerweather and Ladew, tannery
    F. Hady, bakery
    J.W. Hickman, hotel
    John W. Hockman, dentist
    Abraham King, general store and saloon
    George M. Miller
    L.P. Noland, green grocer
    J. Neal Oliver, general store
    Mrs. P.A. Oliver, millinery
    B. Parsons, general store
    J.N. Robinson, general store
    Mrs. M. Sleeth, millinery
    J.M. Smith & Co., furniture and hardware
    M.R. Tavuer, druggist
    A. Thompson, lumber and sawmill
    Wagner and Sutton & Co.
    O.S. Wilson & Bro., general store
    Harry N. Wardon, hotel

6. Dobbins -- (Grant County with Fairfax, Tucker Co. post office box) (population 100)
      J.L. Rumbarger Lumber Co.

7. Forsyth (see William)

8. Hannahsville -- Philippi Banking Town (population 10)
      Claud J. Loughery, jeweler
      Loughery & Bro., grocer

9. Hendricks -- Philippi Banking Town (population 100)
      J.W. Bowinan, grocery store
      A.M. Hill, saloon
      W.B. Hill, grocery store
      Hill & Murphy, liquors
      L.W. James Co., grocery store
      W. Pettit & Co., grocery store
      Poling & Dilworth, grocery store

10. Holly Meadows -- Kingwood or Philippi Banking Town (population 75)
      Jos. Parsons, cattle rancher
      Samson E. Parsons, cattle dealer

11. June
      J.H. Beckman, general store
      Bowman & Ridgeway Co., general store
      S.W. Caylor, general store
      P. Constable & Co.
      H.C. McElfish, general store
      G.D. Minnson, general store
      J.T. Poling & Co., general store
      F.M. Skiles, general store
      D.M. Smith, doctor
      Witt & Harper, general store

12. Leadmine -- Philippi Banking Town (population 15)
      Dumire Shingle Co.
      James L. Evans, miller
      T. W. Palmer, general store

13. Parsons -- (population 50)
      J.H. Beckman
      R.T. Griffith & Son, furniture
      Dr. H.T. Harr, physician
      Dr. Johnson, physician
      S. Kaylor & Co., saloon
      B.B. Metheny, groceries
      J.W. Pifer & Co., groceries
      Jas. L. Poling & Co., groceries
      Lee B. Ridgeway, grocery store
      River Boom Manuf. Co., booms
      L. Simmons, hotel
      Wilt Peter & Co., saloon

14. Pheasant Run -- Philippi Banking Town (population 10)
              _____ Bennett, saloon
      F.M. Taylor, grocery store

15. Red Creek -- Philippi or Piedmont Banking Town (population 20)
      A.R. Flanagan, grocery store
      J.G. Flanagan, store
      Mosh and Raines, grocery store

16. St. George -- Philippi or Kingwood Banking Town (population 400)
      William Cayton, dry goods, carpets
      Cheat River Boom and Lumber Co.
      Eli M. Closs, blacksmith
      W.E. Cupp, grocery store
      Dr. E. Harper, lumber
      V.D. Hart, saddler
      Hulings Lumber Co.
      Lipscomb & Bro., Pioneer newspaper
      C.J. Maxwell
      O.O. Miller & Co., dry goods and groceries
      Thomas M. Miller & Co., groceries
      A.C. Minear, lumber
      David S. Minear, grocery store
      J.P. Scott, Tucker Democrat
      J.A. Shaffer, hotel
      D.L. Steadman, dentist
      W.E. Talbott, tannery
      Toy Finley, hotel
      Wilt Peter, saloon

17. Texas -- Philippi Banking Town (population 10)
      Abolism Phillips & Bro., general store
      Elijah Phillips & Son, general store

18. Thomas -- Piedmont Banking Town, (population 300)
      J. Ash & Co., general store
      S.G. Dixon Co., general store
      Daniel Entler, general store
      W.A. Feely, general store
      Miss M. Hepburn, groceries
      O.H. Huffman, physician
      E.G. Huffman, physician
      Schilansky & Schatz, general store
      Mrs. R.A. Silcott, hotel

19. William -- Piedmont Banking Town (population 30)
      R.R. Somerville, general store and hotel
      B.L. Somerville, lumber company and sawmill

~Tucker County's Role in the Civil War~

Seneca Trail, Corrick's Ford
Battlefield -- postcard, June 1861.
Courtesy of Ray and Lucille Adams.

Isaac (1836-1919) and Lucinda Teter
(1839-1926) Mullenax. Isaac was a
Civil War veteran.
Courtesy of Delain Mullenax.

Seneca Trail, view of Corrick's Ford Battlefield
near Parsons, June 1861, postcard.
Courtesy of Chris Kidwell.

Mike Bodkins, (1842-
1926), married Rebecca
Cooper, b. 1837, farmer
by trade. A private dur-
ing the Civil War in the
62nd Virginia Infantry.
Children: Isaac L., b. 1866,
John Wm., b. 1869, Chas.
L., b. 1872, and Benjamin,
b. 1877.
Courtesy of Steve Bodkins.

Corrick House on Lovers' Lane, U.S. Route 219,
in Parsons, where General Robert S. Garnett died
-- postcard.
Courtesy of Chris Kidwell.

Abe Bonnifield, 1837-1890, Horseshoe Run, Tucker County. Served in the Confederate Army; was born without legs. Little girl is a Hansford.
Courtesy of Chris Kidwell.

Brig.-Gen. Robert Selden Garnett

Ezekiel Harper, 1823-1892, Parsons.
Courtesy of Chris Kidwell.

Robert Selden Garnett was born at Champlain, Essex County, Virginia, December 16, 1819. He graduated from the West Point Military Academy in 1841 and served with auspicious gallantry in the Mexican War. At the outbreak of the Civil War, he resigned from the United States Army and joined the Confederacy. He was made Brigadier General and took command of Confederate troops in Northwestern Virginia, June 14, 1861, at Huttonsville, (West) Virginia. He was killed by musket fire at Corrick's Ford (now Parsons, WV) July 13, 1861 and is buried in New York City beside his wife and son.

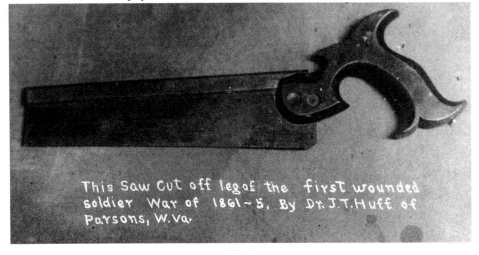

"This saw cut off leg of the first wounded soldier, War of 1861 - 5. By Dr. J.T. Huff of Parsons, W.Va." Postcard -- Surgery was performed June 4, 1861, in Beverly, in the home of J. (N. or W.) Logan. Photo by Broadwater Art Studio.
Courtesy of Chris Kidwell.

Monument commemorating the Battle of Corrick's Ford at the Tucker County Courthouse, July 13, 1861. *Courtesy of Chris Kidwell.*

Samuel Frances Harsh (May 1, 1836 - Jan. 10, 1912), Davis. Son of Jacob and Sarah Stemple Harsh. Married Louisa Nestor. Samuel served with Captain Haller's Home Guard in Barbour County. *Courtesy of Chris Kidwell.*

View of Corrick Battlefield, June 1861, Seneca Trail near Parsons. *Courtesy of David and Rita Roberts.*

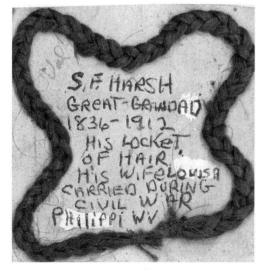

Louisa Nestor Harsh (Dec. 31, 1839 - July 31, 1922), with daughter Amelia. Wife of Samuel, married 1859, Davis. Daughter of Jonas Nestor. Above is photo of Samuel's hair braided for Louisa to keep during the Civil War. *Courtesy of Chris Kidwell.*

Jacob (Jan. 2, 1801-1888) and Sarah Harsh (Dec. 23, 1799 - Dec. 20, 1878). Parents of S. F. Harsh. *Courtesy of Chris Kidwell.*

Devastating Floods
of Tucker County

The home *at the left*, on Pennsylvania Avenue in Parsons,
as flood waters first appeared on Monday night, November 4, 1985.
Photo by Faith Anne Smith Robinson.

Tuesday morning (November 5, 1985) most of the water had receded;
Brocks' back porch and garage were gone.
Photo by Faith Anne Smith Robinson.

Photos by
Faith Anne Smith Robinson.

The John Wilson apartment building on Pennsylvania Avenue, Parsons, Nov. 4, 1985.

By Tuesday (Nov. 5, 1985) the front wall of the building had been ripped away and the avenue was littered with debris.

Overflow from the Black Fork River surrounding the Plumley home in Parsons. Ed Plumley standing on the porch.

Photos by
Faith Anne Smith Robinson
November 5, 1985.

Overflow from the Black Fork River between the Ed and Lola Plumley and George and Mariwyn Smith homes on Pennsylvania Avenue in Parsons.

The Fike and Smith homes, on Pennsylvania Avenue. The Fike home, like more than a dozen homes on Pennsylvania Avenue, was destroyed. The Smiths lost a wrap-around porch and a two-car garage.

Looking east on Pennsylvania Avenue.

1985 Flood Damage at McClain
Printing Company, Parsons.
Courtesy of McClain Printing Company.

Greenlief-Combs Funeral Home and
A&P Store, days after the 1985 flood,
Parsons.

The interior of Greenlief-Combs Funeral
Home after the flood in 1985, Parsons.

Flood of 1985 -- St. George
Courtesy of Ray and Lucille Adams.

Flood of 1985 -- St. George. Elmer Sturms' house, *at the left*.
Courtesy of Jane Pifer.

Flood of 1985, St. George.
Courtesy of Jane Pifer.

Old Sumie Phillips'
House, now owned
by Carricos. Right side
of St. George Bridge
Nov. 4-5, 1985 -- water
half way up the second
floor.
Courtesy of Jane Pifer.

Flood of 1985, St. George. Home
of Mr. and Mrs. Vittie Lipscomb.
Courtesy of Jane Pifer.

Flood of 1985, St.
George. New bridge
across Cheat River.
The old bridge which
stood adjacent to it,
but was no longer in
use, was destroyed.
Courtesy of Jane Pifer.

Index

Episcopal Church 325
Erhard, Martha Caroline Reid 296
Erhard Bros. Jewelry Store 319
Eschelman, Mildred 334
Essex County, Virginia 380
Esso Station 56
Evans, Amber 89
Evans, Barbie 89
Evans, Charles Austin 159
Evans, Daniel "Chopper" 89, 90
Evans, David Crawford 161
Evans, Elliot Franklin 159, 160, 161
Evans, Elmer 159, 161
Evans, Freeman 159, 161
Evans, Greg 101, 105
Evans, James L. 376
Evans, Josh 89, 90
Evans, Lilly Jane 159
Evans, Mabel Knotts 58
Evans, Martha Ellen Smith 159, 160, 161
Evans, Naomi 146
Evans, Natalie 89
Evans, Olive Calhoun 161
Evans, Orpha May 159
Evans, R.W. 10
Evans, Ryan 90
Evans, Virgie Olive 159
Evans, W.H. 375
Evick, Bill iv
Evick, Dick 108
Evick, Linda iv
Eye, Rex 101, 105
Eye, Robin 101
Eye, Steve 101, 105

F

F. S. Johnsons's Drugstore 129
Fairfax 243
Fairfax Avenue 298
Fairfax District 243, 283
Fairfax Stone 243
Fairmont 311
Falkenstine, George 158
Falkenstine, Gladys 158
Falkenstine, Mrs. 158
Fankhouser Handle Factory 49
Fansler, Gerald Lee Verne 64
Fansler, Henry 225, 229
Fansler, Homer Floyd iii, 1, 64, 141,
    189, 225, 243
Fansler, Paul 83
Fansler, Slim 268
Fansler, Stephen Truman 64, 249
Fansler, Wilda 146
Farmers' Institute 113, 114
Fauschenberger, John 299
Fawley Building 75, 118, 119
Fayerweather and Ladew 375
FDR 40
Feely, W.A. 377

Felton, Andrea 98
Felton, Joanna 110
Felton, John 98
Felton, Kennie 101
Felton, Margaret Ann 105, 110
Felton, Mark 98, 101, 105
Ferguson, Hoy (or Roy) 20
Fifth Street 296
Fike 385
Filler, Charles "Pete" 82, 140
Fink, Denny 83
Finley, Toy 377
First National Bank 37, 233
First Street 2, 6, 8, 9, 14, 16, 17, 35,
    37, 85, 119, 121, 123, 127
First United Methodist Church 36
Fisher, Anna 275
Fisher, Charlie 225
Fisher, Frank 275
Fisher, Frank J. 275
Fisher, Hellena 275
Fisher, John 275
Fisher, Katie 275
Fitzwater, Ruby 158
Flanagan, A.R. 377
Flanagan, Boyd 367
Flanagan, J.G. 377
Flanagan, Jacob 31
Flanagan, John S. 31
Flanagan, Laura Sturms 31
Flanagan, Lejoy 78
Flanagan, Little Jim 369
Flanagan, Miss 107
Flanagan, Nora 114
Flanagan, Stuart 367
Flanagan Hill 365, 366, 369
Flanagan Hill/Red Creek School 368
Flanagan Hill Church 369
Flynn, Kenneth 83
Ford's Store 15
Ford F800 American LaFrance 83
Fork Mountain 39, 115
Forsyth 376
Fortney, Reverend Paul 96
Fort Minear 143, 144
Fourth Street 94, 294, 295, 297
Fox, H. 81
Fox, Philip 337
Fraley Place 362
France 20, 31
Frazee, Julie 97
Freeman, Lucille 109
Freeman, Maurice 105
Free Methodist Church 325
Friend, Ally 153
Friend, Jessy 153
Friend, Robert 153
Front Street 8, 247, 249, 251, 263, 269
Frum, Mary Alice 105, 110
Funkhouser, Joan 110

G

Gable, Judy 67
Gailey, Wade 241
Gainer, Dave 147
Garnett, General Robert Selden 379, 380
Gatrell, Dave 125
Gatrelle, William 78
Gaynor, Malone 338
Gehman, Debbie Wilson 101
Gehman, Dennis 101
General Store 320
George, Sally Ann English 66, 67, 109
Germany 56, 318
Getty, Michael A. 246
Getz, E.J. 63, 119
Gilbert, Gwen Mullenax 59
Gilmore, Delbert 52
Gilmore, Grace Goff 122
Gilmore, Jack 103
Gilmore, William 78
Gladwin 345, 348, 349, 362
Glessner, Kathy 101
Godden, Jack 82
Godwin, Mona 242
Goff, Eppilonia 361
Goff, Katorah 96, 122
Goff, Patty 23, 109, 125
Goff family 194
Goff Town 189
Goff's 189
Good, Annie 98
Good, Debbie 98
Good, Donald 103
Good, Donna 98
Good, Granville 80, 168
Gorman, Ted 241
Goss, Brewner 273
Goss, David 273
Goss, Leo 80, 122
Goss, Mary E. 273
Goss, Roy 273
Grafton 92
Grandstaff, Millie 357
Gray, Ancile 108
Gray, Buck 120
Gray, Marg 120
Gray, Pat 120, 140
Gray, Virginia 98
Great Council of West Virginia Improved
    Order of Red Men 203, 204
Green, Darlene Pine 101
Greenlief, Jennifer Jones 140
Greenlief-Combs Funeral Home 386
Greenlief Funeral Home 99
Green Mountain 214, 215, 347
Greider, Ruby 100
Gribble, Pat 101, 105
Griffith 351
Griffith, Don 103

White, Kay Lynn 98
White, Kevin 83, 84, 89, 90
White, Laban 349
White, Mary Ann (James) 170
White, Meril 170
White, Robert 184
White, Russell 170
White, Susan 373
White, William 370
Whitehair, Shane 223
White Ridge 170
Whitt, Sandra 105
Whobrey, Frankie 140
Widemire, E.C. 299
Wiles, Everett 148
Wiles, Gilbert 148
Wiles, Red 338
Wilfong, Brian 98
Wilfong, C. 84
Wilfong, Craig 123
Wilfong, Curt 98
Wilfong, Curtis 101
Wilfong, Diane 98
Wilfong, Kim Michael iv, vi, 50, 101,
    105, 119, 122, 124
Wilfong, Lisa Mauzy Stevens
    vi, 101, 104, 105, 124
Wilfong, Nick 119, 124
Wilfong, S. Craig Sr. 84
Wilhem, Frank 337
William Avenue 291, 294, 296
Williams, Dayton 171
Williams, Effie 171
Williams, Jessie   171
Williams, Ray 171
Williams, S.D. 119
Williams, Senator Bob 223
Williams, Willis 110
Wilson, Clarence 39
Wilson, Dr. N. McK. 299
Wilson, Dr. Noah 295
Wilson, John 122, 384
Wilson, Raymond 103
Wilson, Wade 337
Wilson Lumber Company 61
Wilt, Carolyn June Lambert 97
Wilt Peter & Co. 376
Wimer, Curtis 140
Wimer, Harper "Doc" 108
Wimer, Lee 370
Wimer, Ralph 103, 106, 108
Wimer, Ralph Jr. 100, 102
Windell, Miss 334
Wine, Charlie 130
Wingfield, Billy 103
Wise, Miss 107
Witt & Harper 376
Wolf, Clara "Jill" 23
Women's Temperence Movement 96
Wood, Ruth 109

Woods, James 315, 316, 350, 370
Worden's Hotel 322, 344
Worden's Hotel Restaurant 317
Works Progress Administration 125
World War I 6, 12, 20, 29, 202, 275
World War II 18, 36, 50, 57, 63, 71,
    117, 119, 120, 357, 358
Wotring, Villa 170
Wright, David 160
Wright, Floyd 316
Wright, Rachel McClain 123
WV Central and Pittsburgh Railroad 294
WV Central and Southern Railroad 235
WV Photo Company 98
Wyford, Junior 119
Wymer, Solome Cooper 346
Wymer, William Lee 346
Wyoming 160

Y

Yawkey Lumber Company 202
YMCA Camp Horseshoe 137, 138
Young, Adam 89
Young, Ashley 89
Young, Jean 146
Young, Kelly 89
Young, Randy 89
Young, Robert 146